Exploring Classical Music

A PLEASANT JOURNEY
FOR NOVICE AND EXPERT

Exploring Classical Music

A Pleasant Journey for Novice and Expert

This edition was produced for on-demand distribution by Digitz.net for SuperiorBooks.com, Inc.

For information address:
Digitz.net
731 Wentworth Street
Charleston, South Carolina 29401
www.digitz.net

ISBN: 1-931055-11-4

Printed in the United States of America

Cover Design Copyright © 2000
Lynn Hodges

Exploring Classical Music

A PLEASANT JOURNEY
FOR NOVICE AND EXPERT

Robert Finn

Superior Books

Exploring Classical Music

A PLEASANT JOURNEY
FOR NOVICE AND EXPERT

DEDICATION

For Mary, Larry, Elaine, John, Matthew, Ginny and Sarah.

Table of Contents

PREFACE

This book of essays on great composers is primarily intended for the layman rather than for the already experienced listener or the professional musician, but even the expert should find pleasure in seeing his favorites pass in review.

The reader I have most in mind is someone, perhaps, just beginning to take an interest in classical music, but finding the whole subject rather off-putting, even frightening. Such a person finds the technical terminology daunting, the habitual use of foreign language phrases discouraging, the whole enterprise surrounded by an air of exclusivity and mystery. Much of that air of mystery may even seem to him the deliberate creation of a band of elitist initiates, seemingly bent on keeping the uninitiated at arms length.

But in spite of all this, he (or she) thinks there may be something genuinely attractive in the world of classical music. He has heard a piece somewhere, whether by accident or design; someone special in his life turns out to be a concertgoer; a friend has recommended a recording; he finds himself contracted to attend a concert; there was something classical on a movie sound-track that piqued his interest. In one way or another, a door has opened a crack and the prospect beyond it looks inviting.

I think there are a lot of people like that "out there" — but they don't know where or how to start. The whole subject seems to them arcane, open only to initiates who have studied in secret places and speak a daunting special language.

This is a sad and potentially dangerous situation. "Classical" concert music and opera need all the friends they can get these days. A deadly combination of forces — political, economic, cultural, educational — has isolated these things from a lot of people who might otherwise find them a wondrous addition to their lives. The cultural tide is running against them. They are no longer considered what they once obviously were — a vital part of our human heritage.

Obviously, someone should "do something." That is why I have written these essays.

If, as the pundits tell us, we live these days in a single "global village," then the world of classical music seems to inhabit a forbidding castle on a mountainside some distance out of town. It is surrounded by a moat; banners with strange devices fly from its turrets; and local legend has it that there are warriors poised with vats of boiling oil on the rooftops to repel outsiders who might like to get inside. Entrance doors are few and closely guarded. Yet, night after night, there float out through the open windows the most ravishing, beguiling, beautiful sounds. The passerby listens enchanted, but then looks at the dark, unapproachable place, shrugs and passes on.

What I want to do in these essays is to show where some of those entrance doors are, and to bribe those guards to go off for a drink somewhere while I invite you inside.

My approach is purely musical, through the men who

wrote some of that lovely music. I have written about composers who meet two criteria: (1) their music is often encountered on concert programs, in record shops and in broadcast concerts; (2) their music means something special to me personally.

I have tried to concentrate on the music itself — what makes it distinctive, how it may be heard to best advantage, why it is special. In most cases I have tried to recommend specific pieces, and most especially pieces other than the most commonly heard standard repertory items. The best-known pieces by these composers are readily available in concert and on records; but there are lesser-known works just as well worth knowing. There are lots of fascinating rooms in that castle, and not all of them are easily found by the unguided listener.

This approach is rather similar to the one I adopted in writing Sunday "think pieces" as a daily newspaper music critic for 28 years — but here I need not worry about the draconian space limitations that constantly bedevil everyone who writes about the arts for an American newspaper. You might think of these essays as The Revenge of the Liberated Critic.

I have almost totally dispensed with biographical data, except in cases where it clearly impacts on the music itself. The shelves of libraries and bookstores groan with a vast assortment of biographical books, from dictionaries to full-length scholarly studies. My purpose is mainly to simply introduce you to these composers and to point out things about them and their music that I find extraordinary. The approach is totally and unapologetically personal. If I could put my purpose in a single phrase it would be to make you want to hear this music.

The list of composers treated is also purely personal and entirely arbitrary. There are obvious omissions, which it would be tiresome to list and justify. I have made some obvious choices — Mozart rather than Haydn, Brahms rather than Schumann, Mahler rather than Bruckner, Debussy rather than Ravel. I can only plead that I have restricted myself to composers who have spoken to me over many years as a concertgoer with a peculiarly urgent voice. The list makes no pretense to completeness. My hope is only that it will get you started.

I have had to restrain my own great enthusiasm for some composers whose music I love, but who do not show up terribly often in our musical life these days (Delius, Poulenc, Nielsen, Crumb).

I have also included under the title "Interludes" a series of reflections on some of the problem areas and pressure points that seem important to the world of classical music today. The whole subject of opera, for example, frightens many people who do not know much about it; and the field so loosely designated as "modern" music (by which some people really mean anything later than Richard Strauss or Stravinsky, both of them many years in their graves) needs to be opened up to more and better-equipped listeners.

I hope this book may be a small contribution toward fighting the gloomy malaise that seems to be enveloping the field of classical music in these dawning years of the twenty-first century. We hear about the disappearance of music instruction from our schools, the graying of the concert audience, the deepening financial crises of major performing institutions, the flattening of classical record sales, the loss of common musical literacy, the decline of classical music on the radio. You can almost see the white-robed prophets parading outside our concert halls with their doomsday placards: The End Is Near!

I do not believe this. Change is in the air and change will certainly happen — but the music, one of the great treasures of our short human tenancy on this planet — will survive. There will always be an audience for The Marriage of Figaro, Die Winterreise and the Symphony of Psalms. People need only to be led to these transcendent works by a kindly hand. They do not need to be browbeaten by hectoring academics or mystified by elitist initiates. They need to be given a gift, and shown how to unwrap it.

I hope the approach I have taken may be found useful. One thing I know already — it has been very useful to me. I have had to rethink my attitudes on many questions, and to justify afresh notions that had been lying at the bottom of my mind unquestioned for years. If you learn something by reading these reflections, be assured that I have indeed learned plenty by writing them.

ROBERT FINN

THE LISTENING EXPERIENCE

Music is probably the most difficult of all the arts to experience fully. You can't see it the way you see a painting; you can't touch and feel it the way you might a sculpture or a piece of pottery; there is no visual component fully integrated into it as there is in the theater; there is no physical object analogous to the printed book that mediates between the creator of the message and the one who receives that message. Music is an invisible thing, apprehended through the ears alone. The instruments and players you see onstage at a concert are means to an end, not that end itself.

So it is not surprising that a vast deal of well-meant nonsense — not including, I hope, the present chapter — has been written about "how to listen to music." A sort of cottage industry has sprung up in the name of "music appreciation" (Virgil Thomson memorably branded it "the music appreciation racket"). People who have no interest in or experience of "classical music" look upon those who do as possessors of some sort of mysterious

Rosicrucian knowledge that is denied to lesser mortals.

Music is, however, no different from the other arts in one obvious respect: the more you know about it the more you will get out of the experience. There is nothing wrong — and everything right — with learning as much as you can about music — its technical side, its history, and its esthetic foundations.

This may not be quite so obvious a bromide as it seems, for we live in an age when this kind of serious study is often looked down upon. Many people these days feel that you are supposed simply to wallow in music unthinkingly, to experience what one critic has dubbed mere "idiot sound" instead of learning something about it. Lots of people do that and seem perfectly happy at it. The idea is to simply sit there and let the music "wash over you," give you "a mental bath," without making any effort to know it any better.

Recently I heard a highly respected, intelligent and well-educated man say in a public speech: "I go to a lot of concerts, but I don't really know what I'm hearing." It took some courage to say that in public; many people who go to a lot of concerts might only admit to it in their more honest private moments.

This sort of admission means that the listener is merely experiencing music on the most rudimentary level. Actually, however, the act of listening to music can be far more complicated than that. My thesis is that far greater and more lasting rewards await the listener who comes to music with a background that will help him meet and experience it on a deeper level.

Two things should be added to that premise at once: first, this work "at a deeper level" in no way diminishes or gets in the way of the sheer sensual pleasure of the surface sound of the music; rather, it adds to it. second, music exists on all levels of complexity; some pieces require more of the listener than do others. The level of background required for full enjoyment of, say, a Johann Strauss polka is far less than that required in order to confront a Mahler symphony or Bach's Art of the Fugue.

How do people arrive at this "deeper level" of enjoyment? Do you have to attend a conservatory and earn a degree to do so? Certainly not. Everyone goes about it his own way. Some people do it entirely by accident, entirely unaware of the adventure they are setting out on even while it is happening to them. One of the greatest things about the whole process is that it is so exciting and enjoyable that the adventurer becomes very quickly an enthusiast; the process takes on a life of its own, and it never stops.

As just one representative method among many for getting oneself deeper inside great music, let us consider the matter of "form" as it applies to music.

Some people are surprised to hear that most musical compositions have have "form" in much the same sense that a statue or a painting has "form." Writing a symphony is not simply a matter of starting to compose music and then stopping when you reach the 45-minute mark. There are procedures and rules — not inflexible rules, to be sure, but pre-existing rules that have served other composers well down through the years. There are molds into which a composer may, if he chooses, pour his musical ideas. The composer is free to use these molds as he receives them, to vary them in all sorts of ways, or even to scrap them and make up his own rules; but the point is that a musical composition is not, in the vast majority of cases, just a formless blob of sound but a coherent organization of musical ideas.

The two basic principles that govern musical form are principles so simple that many listeners probably never think about them: repetition and contrast. Repetition gives the listener a sense of familiarity when he hears the return of a theme that he has heard before, either in its original form or in some slightly varied but still recognizable variant. Contrast lends music that sense of variety without which it would quickly lose our interest.

Reducing these ideas to their simplest terms: in the course of a single piece — be it a three minute song or a fifty-minute symphony, a skillful composer makes us say(1) "Here is an interesting idea;" (2) "Oh, here is another, rather different idea;" (3) "Well, well — here is that first idea back again, and I remember it," thus combining the two ideas of repetition and contrast into a single effective musical experience. This is music as a formal structure.

By way of example, the first movements of most

classical-era and romantic-era symphonies are built upon this principal. The three main divisions of such movements are called Exposition, Development and Recapitulation. In the Exposition, two or more contrasting ideas ("themes") are introduced — and sometimes the Exposition is then literally repeated. In the Development, those ideas are "played with" by the composer — varied, contrasted, explored in a whole variety of ways; in the Recapitulation the Exposition is repeated, but with certain subtle changes that combine the ideas of repetition and variation (contrast). You don't really need to know all the fancy technical terminology, but you should be aware of the process.

You can hear this process with crystal clarity in the first movements of most symphonies, for example, by Haydn or Mozart. You can still follow it in the Beethoven symphonies, though here already begins the process of enlarging, elaborating and complicating the process as the imagination and daring of a great pathbreaking composer gets hold of the "rules" and begins bending them out of shape. You can follow the further elaboration of this process in the symphonies of Brahms, Schumann and Schubert. If you want to hear this particular formal scheme inflated (some would say "bloated") to the proportions of a fifty-minute piece, try Richard Strauss's tone-poem Ein Heldenleben, which does exactly that.

There are other formal schemes commonly used by the great composers too: three-part (A-B-A) song form (easily tagged as a variation on the Exposition-

Development-Recapitulation idea), rondo form, variation form, and so on.

Continuing, for the sake of illustration, with this notion of form as a means of gaining deeper knowledge of music, the listener may well be led to notice one of the chief ways by which composers achieve contrast in their music — a prime means of setting off one idea from another. This is the matter of key relationships.

Many lay listeners do not really understand the idea of "key" in music. Simply put, it is a matter of which one among the 24 scale patterns available to a composer in our modern system of tuning is to be used as the basis for a given work or section of a work.

Things get just a bit technical here for a paragraph or two. There are 24 possible scale patterns because there are 12 notes in a chromatic scale (any 12 adjacent notes —white and black keys on a piano), ascending or descending. It doesn't matter which note you start on — under our modern system of tuning if you play 12 adjacent notes on a piano you have played a chromatic scale in some key or other. That accounts for 12 keys; the number doubles to 24 when you add the factor of "major" or "minor" scales — standard variations in the sequence that, to our western ears at least, affect a scale's character. To adopt a useful but dangerous oversimplification, "major" scales usually have connotations of happiness, "minor" scales of sadness.

All this may seem like rather heavy weather for the average untutored listener; the bottom line is that we hear differences in key whether we recognize them or not. Sudden changes of key within a piece give us a sense of "Hey, we are going off in a new direction here. We have turned a corner." The piano sonatas of Schubert are a treasure house of unexpected — and therefore surprising — key shifts. Schubert is famous for shifting not into the keys that are easiest to reach from where he started, but instead into those that are more remote. As has been noted previously, this gives his key-shifts (the technical term is "modulations") a sense of utter unexpectedness that bothers some pedants even to this day. Such people say this disconcerting habit is due to Schubert's supposedly sketchy formal training as a young man. Hogwash, say the rest of us — this is simply a uniquely original and daring genius's way of doing things. If we are not yet "used to it," that just proves how original and daring the man was.

Several of these points can be handily illustrated by referring to a single well-known piece of concert music.

Everybody knows Maurice Ravel's Bolero. (premiered in 1928). Its popularity has extended far beyond the walls of concert halls – an extraordinary achievement for music so comparatively "recent." Bolero has become a part of popular culture.

At first blush, this piece would seem to be the absolute negation of everything we have been talking about. How can you talk about contrast in a piece that consists entirely of a single two-part melody repeated eleven or twelve times with no change in speed, in a single unvarying rhythm and, until the very end, no change of key whatever? There is little or no contrast even between the two strands that make up that two-part melody.

But there is contrast here in plenty. In what? In the orchestration — that is to say, in Ravel's ideas as to which instrument or combination of instruments will play the melody and handle the accompanying rhythm. This was Ravel's daring idea — to forsake all other means of contrast except instrumentation and its inevitable yokefellow, volume of sound. His genius lies squarely in his making this supposedly straight-jacketing experiment work superbly, brilliantly — like those fellows who have written whole novels without using the letter E. The variety in this piece lies in waiting to see which instrument or combination of instruments will take up the melody, and the insistent accompaniment, next. We begin with merely a soft tattoo on the snare drum and the melody disclosed by a solo flute; but as the piece progresses other instruments are added, on both melody line and accompaniment. What began almost inaudibly swells slowly, gradually to a wicked tumult of sinuous sound. Tempo remains absolutely rigid; the rhythm is unchanging; the melody is simply repeated, never varied in the slightest except in its instrumental dress.

Ravel himself once referred to this extraordinary piece slightingly as "twenty minutes of orchestral tissue without music." He was not the first — nor will he be the last — composer to mischaracterize his own music.

But what about key? There is absolutely no change of key through the whole piece until we reach the last few bars, at the height of the sinuous dance, when Ravel does shift, from his unvarying C major into the remote area of E major for the last twenty seconds or so of the piece, which amount to a raucous crash and collapse into exhaustion. He demonstrates his skill here in two ways: first by withholding the key-change as long as possible, thus building up the listener's feeling that (a) it may never change, or (b) it's got to change. This feeling may be unconscious on a listener's part, but it's there; and secondly, by shifting without any advance warning or preparation of any kind, and not into a nearby key but into one quite distant from the key that had been so firmly established over 15 minutes of music.

This technique of shifting from one key to another is a classic skill that composers learned in school in the old days when the tonal system reigned unchallenged. They devoted much time to learning the art of smoothly leading the listening ear from A to B — or perhaps from A to Q or X. It was a standard subject, a trick of the trade that had to be mastered before you could really call yourself a composer. It is still an important matter, even in this day when the tonal system has been dismissed by many composers (but by few listeners) as outdated. Ravel's coup at the end of Bolero was simply to make the key-shift without any effort to forewarn the listener at all, to ambush our ears in a totally surprising and absolutely effective way. It is masterly — as effective on the hundredth hearing as on the first.

Lots of sophisticates dismiss poor old Bolero these days as nothing more than a piece of trickery, a stunt. But it has lessons to teach us.

Well, then: form, repetition, contrast, development, key patterns, key-shifts, instrumentation. These are just a few of the most obvious weapons composers have in their technical arsenal that we can learn about to our own profit as listeners. There are dozens of others, and there are scores of ways of encountering and mastering them without the need to attend conservatory classes. They cannot all be adequately treated within the scope of this essay.

It should be emphasized, too, that none of them will have any real effect on ears that are not really listening. This is not quite the self-evident bromide it may seem on first reading, for we live, alas, in an age when the idea of listening to music with close and undivided attention is, to put it mildly, unfashionable. The plague of "background music" has spread from elevators and restaurants into almost every corner of daily life into home, office and even church.

This is one of the things, for example, that is wrong with classical-music radio these days. Its purveyors readily admit that very few of their listeners are paying undivided attention to what they are broadcasting. Many listeners, for example, are in their cars rather than at home. And the classical stations program with that fact in mind. Just ask them — they will readily admit it, with the air of someone wearily explaining the "facts of life" to a child.

At the risk of riding off Quixote-like to fight a battle that was lost long ago, I must stand up for the idea that listening to great music demands a listener's full attention; it is not something that goes along with eating, reading, conversation, sex or the preparation of tax returns.

This is one of the great advantages of the live concert over radio broadcasts or recordings — it sets the stage for real attention to the musical message, if the listener is willing to summon it. It is at least a little harder to daydream or sleep in a concert hall setting, where strangers (or acquaintances!) can take due notice.

One further point, perhaps the most important of all: the best course of study in getting to know great music is the one you devise for yourself, not one you find laid out in a book or a classroom course. The world of classical music is so wide, so varied and so constantly renewed by new infusions that there is no way any single mentor can systematize it all for you. And there is, to be frank, no way that you (or I) can ever know all of it.

You have to learn for and by yourself , and that is where the joy begins. Great music is not really an academic pursuit — it is an adventure. You can seek guidance (I hope you find some in this book!) but in the end you have to draw your own map, develop your own taste. If you hear something that appeals to you, whether it is the music of Josquin des Pres or John Corigliano, follow it up, seek more music by that same composer, or from that same period. Build your own taste, find enthusiasms (and maybe a few betes noires) for yourself. Do not let anybody put you down for liking (or not liking) something that they like (or dislike). The musical universe is wide enough to accommodate everybody's taste.

There is no greater joy in the world of art than stumbling completely unawares on some piece of music that stops you in your tracks with its urgency, its sincerity, its simple appeal or its sheer sonic beauty. It is like suddenly discovering a new country; it is certainly making a new and lifelong friend.

There is also great joy in coming back later in life and with wiser ears to some piece you thought you knew and discovering things in it that you never knew were there. They were there all along, but the best pieces of music — like the most interesting and intriguing of people — do not yield up all their secrets at first acquaintance.

There is also a wondrous sense of adventure in following the newest trends in "serious" music — keeping up with the fascinating, drastic, path-breaking, and sometimes downright alarming things, that today's composers are doing. Composers today, as in all ages, come in all stylistic shapes and sizes. You don't have to like everything you hear — indeed there's something wrong somewhere if you do. They are a fractious and wildly varied lot, but among them are some immense talents. You and I might not agree on which are the talents and which are not, but we can both enjoy the hunt.

Listening to great music — with ears, mind, brain and heart all wide open — can change your life. I know, because it happened to me.

I. PIOTR ILYICH TCHAIKOVSKY (1840-1893)

Of all "classical" composers, Tchaikovsky and Beethoven have made the most impact on people who do not consider themselves classical music listeners. Beethoven has indeed become a kind of cottage industry, promoted by movies, the concocters of TV commercials, the record industry and other sources as the very archetype of the "great" composer. He is probably the one composer who would be unquestioningly accepted as a "great" creator of classical music by both the critic in his concert hall aisle seat and the average citizen sitting behind third base at the ballpark.

Tchaikovsky's celebrity is different. It has been achieved mainly through the emotional appeal of his music itself, rather than through any organized propaganda campaign, commercial or otherwise. His music turns up in all sorts of "crossover" venues where Beethoven's (with the single recent exception of the "Ode to Joy" theme from the ninth symphony) does not penetrate. People who would be scared to death to cross the threshold of a symphonic concert hall know themes from The Nutcracker, the big introductory tune from the B-flat piano concerto, the slow movement of the op. 11 string quartet, the famous love theme from the Romeo and Juliet overture-fantasy and perhaps a tune or two from the Pathetique symphony. Back in the 1940s the pop music industry paid Tchaikovsky the dubious tribute of raiding his works for the raw material of popular songs — something that (hosanna in excelsis!) has never happened on anything like the same scale to Beethoven.

Tchaikovsky has paid a price for the patent surface attractiveness of much of his music — that very quality has held down his reputation among a good many trained musicians. There is a curious but all-too-prevalent attitude at work here, the feeling that because something is extremely popular with a mass audience, it must therefor be an inferior product. This may sometimes be true, of course (it is certainly true with respect to several of Tchaikovsky's own minor works), but that does not make it into some sort of immutable law, applicable in all cases.

The condescending attitude toward many of Tchaikovsky's large-scale works on the part of large numbers of musical professionals seems to me a case in point. Here we have a major composer who by any reckoning has managed at the same time to appeal to a wide spectrum of listeners, including many who are not concertgoers. Far from considering this an excuse for snobbish rejection of the product, I consider it cause for rejoicing. The music of Tchaikovsky seems to me an ideal vehicle for opening the door to classical music and inviting perhaps timorous inquirers inside to the rich and varied banquet that awaits them. That is one reason why this essay on his music stands first in this book.

In certain sophisticated musical salons these days, it takes a certain amount of courage to swim against the critical tide and admit to a genuine liking for Tchaikovsky, but the swim itself is invigorating, and more people ought to try it.

Tchaikovsky led a turbulent and tragic life. Aside from the storms and passions that, almost as a matter of course, often seem to buffet the lives of Russian artists, he was tormented throughout his years by, among other things, the fact of his homosexuality. There was also, of course, his strange arms-length relationship with the wealthy lady patron, whom he never actually met, the Baroness Nadezhda Von Meck. His letters, too, are full of self-doubt.

All of these various interior emotional storms also color his music. They are doubtless the source of the passions that sweep through it so grandly and speak so seductively to ears both musically sophisticated and naive.

His musical fate was also inexorably shaped by his place at the center of another sort of storm, this one purely artistic. He had the bad (or, from posterity's point of view perhaps, good!) luck to live at a time and in a country where artistic battles were being fought between opposing ideologies. The history of Russian music in his time is the history of a conflict between "nationalist" and "cosmopolitan" forces, both wrestling for the musical soul of the country.

The "nationalists," led by the charismatic but now nearly forgotten Mily Balakirev (1837-1910), and including two of the greatest names in Russian music (Moussorgsky and Rimsky-Korsakoff) were calling upon the country to find its musical voice within its own borders by drawing upon the rich lode of Russian folk music, fairy tale, folktale and outright myth, as well as the colorfully bloody pageant of Russian history itself. They were sketchily trained, in some cases almost avocational composers, who nonetheless founded a powerful movement that made a lasting contribution to the world's music.

The other group, many of them trained in the great conservatories of central Europe and steeped in the mainstream musical tradition that those conservatories perpetuated, felt that Russian music had to join and contribute to that mainstream, not veer off into the superficially attractive but ultimately self-defeating backwater of nativist preoccupation. The Rubinstein brothers, Nicolai and Anton, were leading figures in this group.

Tchaikovsky stood pretty much at the center of this historical controversy. Listening to his music, you can hear influences from both sides. Like so many of his countrymen, he was deeply rooted in Russian soil, and he could not stay away from it for very long without actually weeping from sheer loneliness (as he did during his visit to New York in 1891 when he was the celebrity attraction at the opening of Carnegie Hall). But there was also a "cosmopolitan" side to the man's genius, a strain that valued formal perfection and technical polish as highly as it did raw, unfiltered "inspiration." Unlike most of the nationalists, he had traveled a good deal outside of Russia and did not regard mainstream European musical tradition as an alien thing.

With the perspective of history, musicologists have thus classified Tchaikovsky more with the "European" group than with the nationalists, but there is at least some room for debate here. The "nationalists" certainly were suspicious of his loyalties and never really admitted him to their circle. Yet, look at the literary and folkish sources for his operas, for example, or at the obvious native influences at play in his symphonies.

The uncomfortable position that he thus occupied, precariously balanced between two contending camps, was certainly another source of his greatness. The battle raged within himself as it did outside himself, and the tensions it generated helped to make his music great.

This is one of the great sad truths of art: great works seldom seem to arise out of comfortable circumstances; it often takes conflict, uncertainty and tension to release creative impulses. One should ordinarily beware of such generalities, but this one seems to have proved true often enough to earn itself a measure of credibility.

Someone has written too that one important facet of Tchaikovsky's genius was his ability to synthesize the styles of the concert hall and the ballet. He has been credited with writing ballet scores (Swan Lake, Sleeping Beauty) that approach the condition of symphonic music, and symphonic pieces that have obvious roots in dance. A prime example of obviously dance-influenced symphonic music occurs, for instance, in the swaying 9/8 rhythms that pervade much of the first movement of his fourth symphony. The third movement of the fifth symphony is a fetching, symphonically treated waltz. For ballet music of symphonic proportions, you have only to listen to almost any major section of the two popular ballet scores listed above.

For a man whose life was so filled with tragic drama, Tchaikovsky has, in the field of opera, had curiously little success outside his native country. Only two of his ten or eleven operas, Eugene Onegin and Pique Dame, (known in English as The Queen of Spades) have had any substantial success beyond the borders of Russia. Many of his other operas, though available on records, are hardly ever seen on Western stages.

Onegin is an especially puzzling case, for it is a beautiful and effective work, packed with full-throated Tchaikovskyan melody and orchestrated with great subtlety. It is revived quite frequently, and whenever this happens, audiences go and are enchanted with the work. They turn to each other at intermissions and say, "Why isn't this lovely opera heard more often?" No satisfactory answer is ever forthcoming. Then, when the run of performances is over, the opera drops out of sight for a few more years until some genius of an impresario thinks to revive it again, whereupon the audience comes again, is again delighted, and turns to its neighbor at intermission with the same question all over again. This Sisyphean cycle has been going on for well over a century. I have no idea why, unless it is because the tenor gets killed in the second act.

Three of Tchaikovsky's six symphonies have become part of the musical world's common speech; they are, in fact, the subject of one of the conservatory world's hoariest jokes:

Professor in music history class: How many symphonies did Tchaikovsky write?
Student: Three.
Prof: Name them, please.
Student: The fourth, fifth and sixth.

In recent years the second (Little Russian) symphony has been heard a little more often, and the first (Winter Dreams) gets an occasional airing. Both works have much to recommend them. The second symphony in particular is a work worth many more performances than it gets these days; but neither it nor the first symphony has ever come close to challenging the popularity of the "big three" — numbers four, five and six.

What has, in fact, challenged the reign of those

three famous symphonies in the past 40 years or so has been the rise in popularity of Bruckner and Mahler, two symphonists who inhabit, though from vastly different perspectives, the same late-romantic corner of the musical world as do Tchaikovsky and Sibelius. With the invention of the long-playing record about 1947, Bruckner's and Mahler's lengthy symphonies suddenly became easily available to the general public, and Tchaikovsky and Sibelius went into something of a slump in order to make room for the newcomers (The previous neglect of Bruckner and Mahler was not altogether, of course, a matter of their unsuitability for recordings on the old 78-rpm records; it had to do also with outright prejudice among the critical fraternity — but that is another story.)

The three well-known Tchaikovsky symphonies fully deserve their popularity. Though their emotional appeal is immediate, they are not conductor-proof. The fourth in particular can suffer at the hands of a conductor who simply wants to blast out its moments of high passion as loudly and stridently as possible; and the sixth, the famous Pathetique, also suffers at the hands of conductors who feel compelled to out-Tchaikovsky Tchaikovsky, especially in that hyper-emotional last movement. Actually, there is a fair amount of music in the Pathetique that is not particularly "pathetique" at all. The famous march-scherzo third movement seems to me more demonic than anything else, and the extraordinary allegro con grazia second movement has an undeniable ingratiating lilt to its main section, despite the limping 5/4 meter that is sustained throughout; it is dance music that you can't dance to. Even the extraordinary slow sad finale of the Pathetique, though music obviously conceived in personal anguish, does not (at least for me) reach the depth of total crushing hopelessness that strikes like the blow of an axe at the end of Mahler's sixth symphony. Mahler's final musical gesture is a sudden and unexpected catastrophe, the more crushing for its very suddenness.

The finales of these two "tragic" symphonies, by the way, are perfect illustrations of one of the great truths of art. They testify to the fact that a great composer can take sentiments that most of us would find simply unbearable and transmute them through the power of art into something not only compelling but also wondrously beautiful. It is a mystery, but that mystery is touched with genius.

If ever a work has suffered the ill effects of over-popularity it is Tchaikovsky's B-flat piano concerto, unquestionably the most-often-performed of all concer-tos for whatever instrument. Dismissed as crude and unplayable by Nicolai Rubinstein when brand-new (a fate it shared with the composer's now-famous violin concerto), it has gone on to conquer the world. Ironically its most popular feature with the general public — the famous introductory tune that begins the work and then disappears without further trace — has been condemned by musicologists as the concerto's most glaring defect.

Here we have a great, soaring, singing tune, introduced with pompous bravado and thundered at us for four or five minutes (the episode takes up about one fifth of the running time of the entire first movement), which is then simply dropped and never heard from again. One critic (I forget who) compared it to a great-columned Gothic building facade which forms the front to a very modest and unassuming structure behind. But the general listening public could not care less about such academic matters. It still goes away from each performance humming that famous tune.

Another and perhaps even more curious aspect of this piece has received far less attention. I know people who have been listening to this concerto all their lives without noticing that there are two versions of the principal theme of the slow movement. When first heard from solo flute over soft plucked strings at the beginning, the third note of the melody is an F, but at every other recurrence that note goes up to a B-flat, giving the melody a slightly different cast. Some conductors have gone so far as to change the flute solo, assuming that Tchaikovsky made a thoughtless mistake that then somehow went undiscovered by himself, his editors and proofreaders forever after. Not so. He wanted it that way.

Among Tchaikovsky's more popular works, the suite of character dances from The Nutcracker can be recommended as far more than the charming trifles that most people consider them. In addition to being delightful little pieces, they are remarkable examples of Tchaikovsky's skill and subtlety at orchestration; notice, for example, the picturesque use of piccolo over grumbling bassoons in the little Chinese Dance. The Romeo and Juliet overture-fantasy and the fine Serenade for Strings are other pieces whose popularity has been honestly earned.

The same cannot be said, alas, for certain other well-known and often-played Tchaikovsky works — the windblown Manfred Symphony and Francesca da Rimini, the pompous Marche Slav and the unabashedly vulgar Overture, The Year 1812, which Tchaikovsky himself dismissed as a potboiler. Personally, I would add to that list of popular but unworthy pieces one more item, the famous Rococo Variations for cello and orchestra (also often heard for cello and piano), beloved of all cellists. This piece, for all its popularity, is basically a mere showoff stunt for virtuoso cellists. Such pieces - and they are legion — inevitably rank lower on the artistic scale than music that was torn from a composer's gut by the overwhelming inner necessity to express himself.

Among Tchaikovsky's lesser-known works, one worth more frequent revival is the string sextet Souvenir de Florence; and many of his songs ought to be better known than they are.

Tchaikovsky's major compositional gifts were two: the ability to conceive and spin out lovely, sweet-sad melodies that might degenerate into mere sentimentality on the score-paper of a lesser composer, but seldom, if ever, do on his; and a directness of emotional expression which allows him to pour out his feelings onto that score-paper without reserve and without obscuring the emotional message through self-consciously "intellectual" devices. There is plenty of "art" in this music to be sure, but it is art securely in the service of emotional expression. And inevitably there are excesses of emotional expression in his music too, places where he doth protest too much.

I said at the outset that Tchaikovsky may be the ideal composer to give a fledgling listener entree into the world of classical music. True, but that does not mean that that same listener cannot continue to draw inspiration and sustenance from the man's music long after he has graduated from apprentice status to that of senior listener, or whatever. The only real danger with Tchaikovsky's music is that of taking it for granted.

II. LUDWIG VAN BEETHOVEN (1770-1827)

When the developers of the compact disc were refining their product in the early 1980s, they sought a standard for establishing how much music could or should be accommodated on each specimen of the new medium.

They found their answer in the ninth symphony of Beethoven, which they regarded as the quintessential "great" work of classical music. The new discs were thus engineered to carry a complete performance of the ninth — about 65 minutes of music. Some CDs since then have pushed the limit up to around 75 minutes, but the basic standard had been set by a work written some 160 years before the CD was invented.

This fact is emblematic of Beethoven's standing in world culture (not merely world music) these days. Beethoven is the standard by which other composers are judged. He is the chief god in music's pantheon.

Any orchestra facing a financial crisis knows that an all-Beethoven program will always fill the house. Movies are made about him (witness the success of Immortal Beloved, among other examples). The Beethoven literature rivals in size that of Lincoln and Napoleon among non-religious figures. Beginning piano students toil away at Für Elise and world-famous virtuosi do the same over the late piano sonatas. The ninth symphony regularly wins radio listener popularity polls with ease. The fifth symphony's opening motive helped win World War II, and many a maiden has swooned in ecstasy to the strains of the first movement of op. 27, no. 2, the misnamed Moonlight Sonata.

Since Beethoven lived only 57 years, the purveyors of records, books, concerts and music in general were delighted in 1970 to market the 200th anniversary of his birth with a blizzard of Beethoveniana, and then to repeat the same promotions only seven years later to mark the 150th anniversary of his death. Every last scrap of his music, I believe, has long since been recorded, most of it many times over.

Beethoven's popular image is neatly summed up by the caption on a poster that used to hang in my longtime place of employment. The picture was the familiar one of the scowling, defiant composer. The caption over it read:

HE WAS A TITAN, WRESTLING WITH THE GODS.

All of this means simply that the music of Ludwig

van Beethoven is inescapable to anyone who wants to attend classical concerts these days. You have to at least come to terms with it, because you could not avoid it even in the unlikely event that you might want to.

Beethoven was indeed one of those crucial figures in the history of music that changed the art single-handedly (there have been others: Monteverdi, Wagner, Schoenberg). The process by which he led music out of the Classical era, so beautifully epitomized by Haydn and Mozart, and into the Romantic age is readily hearable in his music. It is astonishing to realize that the same hand that wrote the early piano sonatas of op. 2 also wrote the complex and futuristic music of opp. 109, 110 and 111, or that the courtly op. 18 string quartets came from the same brain that later produced op. 135.

I once heard a prominent musician describe the experience of attending a symphony concert at which Beethoven's first three symphonies were performed in chronological order. The Haydnesque grace of the first gave way to the somewhat more unbuttoned good spirits of the second. Then came intermission, after which orchestra and audience reassembled, and the downbeat came for the Eroica. Those two abrupt E-flat major chords that open the piece seemed to sweep away at a stroke the world epitomized by the first two symphonies, and to establish that the Romantic Era had dawned then and there. Even for a listener like this musician, who knew all three pieces intimately, it was an unforgettable music-history lesson.

The problem for many a modern-day listener is that it is simply impossible for us today to listen to Beethoven's music with the same sense of freshness, audacity and adventure that it conveyed to listeners when it was new. We have heard all these famous symphonies, concertos and sonatas too many times to be genuinely surprised any more by what is in them. This process of over-familiarization took a long time to do its work in the case of certain late works - the last string quartets in particular — but it is now a fact. There are no surprises left, and even the new listener coming to these pieces for the first time is weighted down in advance with such an enormous baggage of description, analysis, hagiography and romantic moonshine that he must find it difficult to distinguish his own gut reaction from all that he has been burdened with by the busy magnates of the Beethoven Industry.

During one of the recent Beethoven commemorative years referred to above, I recall someone remarking wisely that if, by some magical process, Beethoven could have been brought back from the dead to witness all that was going on in his name, he would have been both angry and mystified to find his music considered safe and unthreatening. He did not intend for audiences to sit placidly through his iconoclastic, path-breaking pieces without being touched by their musically revolutionary spirit. This is the kind of reaction we cannot easily summon up today, when these pieces are available by the shelf-full in every record shop and are programmed with such frequency in live concerts and on the radio. Their rough edges, so apparent to Beethoven's mystified contemporaries, have been worn smooth for us, except of course for those encountering them for the very first time. (When reproached for his conservative programming, the late great conductor George Szell used to remark on how wonderful it is that in every audience there is always someone who is hearing the Beethoven fifth symphony for the first time.)

One example among hundreds may make the point about "rough edges" clear. When we listen today to the introductory bars of the first symphony, do they strike us as "dissonant," as they did Beethoven's contemporaries? Are we concerned that the piece takes twelve or thirteen bars to finally settle into its advertised home key of C major, as those first audiences were? Do the little ascending introductory flourishes that start the finale disconcert us as they reportedly did those early listeners (at least one conductor of the day is recorded to have regularly omitted them?)

Mr. Szell also summed up this dilemma nicely, though he was speaking at the time about music that predates Beethoven. When we get all through with our scholarly research into notation, period instruments, pitch, performance practice and all the other components of that will-o-the-wisp, "authentic" performance of old music, said Szell, there is one further thing we cannot do: we cannot then "listen with eighteenth-century ears."

The melodramatic details of Beethoven's personal

life are also inextricably bound up with his music in the public's mind. The fact of his deafness, dating from about the time of the second symphony (1802) and leaving him utterly unable to hear for the last third or more of his life, is, to be sure, one of art's great tragedies. It has lent Beethoven an extra halo of tragic grandeur that has in turn reacted back onto the music itself in the minds of many listeners. The famous episode of Beethoven's inability to hear the tumultuous applause of the audience at the premiere of the ninth symphony until one of the solo singers took his arm and turned him around so he could see the audience reaction is certainly one of the great pathetic pictures in the whole history of art.

Listeners today, consciously or not, have factoids like this stored in the backs of their minds as they listen to the music, and inevitably they thus listen differently. It is a very natural human reaction. Who could read the heartbreaking words of Beethoven's Heiligenstadt Testament, which dates from about the time of the second symphony (1802), and not let it color his reaction to the music Beethoven wrote after that date? This was the document in which Beethoven, aged about 32, poured out his despair at the realization of his encroaching deafness.

Composition did not come easily for Beethoven, as it did for Mozart, for example. His voluminous musical sketchbooks have been a mother lode for musicologists since his own day, and they tell a tortured tale of constant revision, false starts, discarded ideas and initial inspirations teased, tortured and hammered at until their final shape could not have been predicted from their first versions. Whether or not he was indeed "wrestling with the Gods," Beethoven was constantly wrestling with his own musical instincts. I find this implicit in his famous reply to his violinist friend Schuppanzigh, who had complained about the technical difficulty of a passage in one of the late works: "Do you really think," said Beethoven loftily, "that I think about you and your miserable fiddle when the spirit moves me and I compose?" These are not the words of one to whom composition was a mere pastime.

If Mozart was a kind of cosmic musical secretary, serenely and effortlessly taking dictation from his Muse, with everything already worked out to the last detail before he took the trouble to write it down, then Beethoven presided over a smoky, noisy musical forge where the finished product came out bathed in his own tears and sweat.

The British critic Martin Cooper had recourse to an obscure term to describe the feeling of storm and stress that informs so much of Beethoven's later music. The feeling, at least for the listener, Cooper said in his fine 1970 book, Beethoven: The Last Decade, is one of nimiety, which my Webster's Unabridged defines as "the state of being too much; excess; redundancy." There is a feeling that Beethoven is trying to make instruments (or voices, fingers, lips) do more than they are naturally capable of. The music seems to want to burst the bonds of normal earthbound emotion and technique. Ask any soprano chorister who has coped with the Missa Solemnis or the ninth symphony.

Cooper is right. This feeling of strain is very definitely a part of some of the late Beethoven works. It is a great advantage for the listener to be there, to see the performer(s) sweating and straining; this sensation is part of the piece. Some of these late pieces thus do not make the same gut-wrenching effect on records that they do in live performance — and as for the modern vogue for electronically synthesized versions where the performer is actually eliminated, out the door along with the missing performer goes an essential element of the whole listening experience.

Every listener will have his personal favorites among the great standard-repertory Beethoven works. There is no point really in rehearsing here the familiar glories of the symphonies, the piano concerti, the violin concerto, the op. 59 quartets, the six or eight best known piano sonatas, the four or five most familiar Beethoven overtures. These pieces are simply inescapable in our concert life today. The Missa Solemnis, the Mass in C and Fidelio would take a whole chapter by themselves to discuss adequately. There is a special joy, however, in exploring some lesser-known aspects of Beethoven's large output, pieces that perhaps are not encountered every day but which will reward careful and frequent listening.

Among the orchestral works, for example, I have

always admired the Consecration of the House Overture, op. 124, a large-scale ceremonial piece that concludes with a brilliant fugue. I arranged for the stately opening theme of this piece to serve as the processional at my wedding, and for the drums-and-trumpets fanfare that follows it to be the recessional piece; both served their purposes superbly.

The famous Grosse Fuge (Great Fugue) movement that concludes the op.133 string quartet is often heard in a string orchestra version or in versions for other instruments; in almost any version — including its original quartet incarnation — I find it an irresistibly powerful piece, perhaps the perfect example of what Martin Cooper meant by "nimiety." Beethoven's publisher seems to have agreed, for he felt that this lengthy piece would be just too much for audiences, coming at the end of a long and difficult string quartet. Beethoven obligingly wrote a less weighty finale to replace it. It was the last piece he ever completed.

Among the piano sonatas, once you have made the acquaintance of the Pathetique, the Moonlight, the Hammerklavier, the Waldstein, the three final sonatas and the various other Beethovenian giants of the genre, take a look at some of the earlier works in the series. They may not be quite so "orchestral" in concept or so philosophically lofty, but they can be utterly charming, especially when you play — or try to play — them yourself. I have always had a sneaking fondness for the little A major sonata, op. 2 no. 2, the one in C minor, op. 10 no. 1, the unjustly neglected smaller-scale pieces opp. 78 and 90, and the E flat, op. 31 no. 3, just to name a few.

Also among Beethoven's piano works there is one giant piece, the Diabelli Variations, op. 120, which is not heard nearly so often as it deserves, largely because of its length and technical difficulty. It is well worth searching out, and will reward the closest kind of listening.

I also enjoy the cello sonata, op. 69 and the charming little quintet for piano and winds, op. 16 — admittedly not a major Beethoven pronouncement, but one that has its own kind of lightweight appeal. The theme of the rondo finale always reminds me of a tune from Mozart's Don Giovanni.

Beethoven wrote a fair number of songs, many of them well worth knowing. The beautiful Adelaide is fairly often heard. Less well known but a truly lovely work is the cycle An die Ferne Geliebte (To the Distant Beloved), the first true song-cycle in the literature.

Fidelio is Beethoven's only opera and the work that, according to his own confession, cost him more trouble than any of his other "children." Many excerpts from this opera have become well known independently of it, as for example Leonora's passionate Abscheulicher! aria, Florestan's aria in the prison scene, and of course the famous Leonora No. 3 overture. But there are other things in this remarkable work that deserve to be better known, including the famous "canon quartet" (Mir Ist so Wunderbar) near the beginning, the great chorus of prisoners that closes the first act, the powerfully pictorial orchestral prelude to the prison scene, and — a special favorite of mine — the wonderful grave digging duet between Leonora and Rocco, a perfect musical realization of hard, laborious work masking stifled emotional turmoil. These are pieces not often excerpted in concert situations and not at all likely to turn up on discs of "favorite" Beethoven excerpts.

Beethoven was not a natural-born melodist like Mozart or Schubert, though some of music's truly great melodies are to be found in his output. A more apposite aspect of his genius was rather a consummate talent for making much out of little, for taking what might seem to be unpromising raw material and constructing wondrous castles with it. The opening movement of the fifth symphony is a famous example of this; the Diabelli Variations provide an even more technically awesome example.

The world has a habit of making marble statues of its heroes, setting them up in public places and then more or less forgetting about them. Not so with Ludwig van Beethoven. He resists marble-ization and continues to speak to us today — if we can remember how to listen to him.

INTERLUDE I: The Early Music Movement

There has probably been no more widely-publicized or influential development in the music world since the end of World War 2 than the dramatic rise of the early music movement — variously dubbed Historical Performance Practice (HIP for short), Period Instruments, or, most controversially, Authenticity.

Simply put, this is a school of thought that seeks to recreate, so far as possible, performances of older music as they were heard at the time of their composition rather than simply performing them today in the same way, and with the same style and the same instruments that we use to perform newer music.

The roots of this idea go back long before World War 2, of course. There have always been individual performers, and even groups, who tried to find out how older music sounded when it was new, and to somehow convey that experience to modern ears. The legendary harpsichordist Wanda Landowska (1877-1959) was perhaps the best known among many early enthusiasts for this "early music" idea. But since 1945 the movement has grown at an incredibly rapid pace, has spread over the entire musical map and has in important ways changed the way we hear music, even music of our own time. That is its importance within the context of this book; for any serious music listener today, this phenomenon is simply unavoidable, so at least some nodding acquaintance with it is essential. It has also, as all such movements do (and not only in music!) given rise to some sharp controversy.

The specifics of this wide-ranging phenomenon take many forms. Questions that arise, and that the scholars try their darndest to answer, include: what sort of instruments was this music really written for? How do they differ from our modern instruments? What were the commonly accepted ideas about tempo at the time of composition? How sacrosanct is the written musical score itself? Was it not understood in many cases that the written page was merely a sketch or guide, and that the performer was expected to improvise decorative embellishments? What about pitch — were not instruments in general tuned to a lower pitch in Mozart's time than they are today? Have not styles of singing changed drastically since those early years? How should a modern singer approach a work from a period long behind him?

Those are just the basics. There are plenty of other considerations.

To put this whole question in an obvious form by use of a familiar example, consider one of the most popular works ever written — Handel's great oratorio *Messiah* (not, by the way, *The Messiah*; the correct title is a single word). For many years this work was heard in performances that involved choruses of several hundred and a large orchestra, usually playing on modern instruments. Tempos were prevailingly slow and the pace somewhat ponderous, with solemn pauses between pieces. This was the English choral tradition of a century or more ago, much beloved by armies of devoted listeners and considered something of a national monument, even a kind of religious experience by some.

Now, however, such performances are rare indeed — virtually non-existent in major musical centers. The scholars tell us the early performances of *Messiah* used a chorus of 25 or so and an orchestra of maybe 20 players, with the aria soloists not separate from the chorus, but drawn from its ranks. Tempos were much quicker. The thing moved. Modern performances that slipped back into the now-discredited older tradition would be savaged by the critics. The old "national monument" style has become a laughing stock, though the work itself remains indestructibly popular.

To add a note of mystification to the question of how the work should be done, the scholars point out gleefully that Handel himself conducted *Messiah* four or five times, and that each performance was different, with changes made in the order of the pieces and in the voice ranges of soloists in some of the arias, depending on the availability and vocal strengths of the singers. So where does the "authentic" Messiah reside?

That is just the single most obvious way to illustrate what has happened. The scholarship that has gone into the early music movement is breathtaking in its extent. Old manuscripts have been restudied; old paintings that show instruments and performances have been painstakingly studied; an entire industry of preserving old instruments or making faithful modern copies has sprung up; old scholarly monographs, letters and newspaper accounts have been unearthed and minutely parsed. There are societies, publications, conferences, whole concert series. Much of what has resulted from this has been lovingly documented on recordings. A fair number of record labels have come into being specifically to further the early music cause.

All this has affected mainstream concert life drastically. Our great modern symphony orchestras seldom play Bach much any more — because they know that if they did this very often using their modern fiddles, flutes and cellos, they would be severely criticized. When they do venture a B Minor Mass or a Saint Matthew Passion they are careful to make at least some attempt at "authentic" performance practice. We hear these great works more and more in performances by specialized early music groups, rather than by mainstream organizations. This is a total reversal of the way things used to be.

Another side effect has been that the frontier of what constitutes "early music" has been steadily creeping forward toward our own time. No longer is the idea of "historical performance" restricted to the Mozart era and earlier. The principle has been extended to the romantic era, and even beyond. There have been pianists who have advertised themselves as giving "authentic" performances of the music of George Gershwin.

Controversy arose at first because there were some in the early music vanguard who simply insisted that they had established something close to an absolute standard for how this music should be performed, and that anything that differed from what they offered, to the extent of the difference, was "inauthentic." They condemned as no longer defensible many a practice that had been the meat and drink of concert audiences for many years — for example, the performance of Mozart piano concertos on modern nine-foot concert grand pianos backed by an orchestra of maybe 50 players using modern instruments. The New Scholarly Gospel was that if you wanted to be "historically correct" you must use a fortepiano of the type for which Mozart actually wrote, and maybe as few as six, eight or a dozen players in the orchestra. (the fortepiano is a kind of halfway house or way station between the harpsichord which was the dominant keyboard instrument up through the Baroque era, and the modern piano, whose development began at about the time of the death of Bach in the late 17th century.)

Modern concert audiences quite naturally rebelled at such an idea, and continued happily to listen to their

Mozart on modern pianos. They still do so today, but they must now share the stage (and the record catalogues) with those fortepianos.

Perhaps that example is a bit of an oversimplification. Most of the early music scholars admitted right from the start that they had not uncovered Absolute Truth. In the first place, exactly what that Absolute Truth was could not really be determined with total accuracy in most cases. It was elusive, shrouded in mist and conjecture. There were, alas, no recordings of how Mozart's orchestra sounded.

The most responsible of these scholars admitted right away that very little was known "for sure" about what they were doing. More often they simply said: "We think this is a pretty good guess at what this music sounded like to the first ears that heard it. We cannot claim absolute certainty, but we do feel that what we are doing comes a lot closer to the real thing than modern performance practice does."

There were some surprisingly sharp (often amusingly sharp!) disputes among the scholars themselves as to what the proper procedures should be in such matters as embellishment of vocal or instrumental melodic lines, the proper execution of signs indicating ornaments, etc. It was not quite the classic dispute over angels dancing on the head of a pin, but it was close enough, so far as the non-specialist listener was concerned, to seem both stuffy and faintly comical.

All of this scholarly ferment was unquestionably a

healthy thing for the art of music. No matter who was "right" or "wrong," it stirred up an awful lot of valuable research into things that really did matter and that deserved to be explored. The dogmatists who insisted that they alone had the Truth were never more than a small noisy minority among the company of responsible scholars; unfortunately, though, they got much of the publicity and formed the image of the whole movement in the minds of many a mainstream concertgoer.

I think, though, that the main value of this whole movement was something quite apart from these stylistic questions, important though they are.

What really mattered, I feel, is that this movement opened up to a much wider public and incredible vast storehouse of wonderful music that had been previously unknown to it. No longer were Bach and Vivaldi considered the earliest composers who amounted to anything. Suddenly there was available, in performance and on records, a whole enormous repertory of vocal music, instrumental music, secular music, church music, folk-inspired music, what-have-you. Whole schools of composition like the English madrigalists or the Netherlands Polyphonists were suddenly open books to a whole new public. Music that even the most open-eared of mainstream listeners had perhaps avoided because it seemed to be the property of dusty historians rather than performers, was suddenly out there in the open for them to listen to and cherish. The rear-guard boundary of available and listenable music was quickly pushed back 600 years or so from the time of Bach and Vivaldi as far as that of Hildegard von Bingen (1098-1179). Think about that — 600 years would encompass all the music written between roughly 1400 and today.

The repertory of music thus brought to light is so vast, the diversity of styles so great, and the questions of performance practice so murky that it is rather futile to single out specific eras, styles, or composers. The whole corpus of music is there for the taking. Every man to his own taste.

This extraordinary expansion of the repertory has also reflected forward to the music of our own time. Many composers, starting from about the time of Stravinsky, have professed themselves influenced by this older music and have reflected it in their own work. Modern composers like Poland's Krzysztof Penderecki and Estonia's Arvo Pärt have consciously reflected it in their own works. Thus the music of a millennium ago has actually exercised an important influence on the music of the late 20th and early 21st centuries — a time of discontent in many quarters with the direction music was taking and a time of searching for new/old paths.

The perceived rivalry between the early music movement and the musical mainstream, it seems to me, is just that — a "perceived" rivalry rather than a real one. As time has gone on, level heads in both camps seem to have achieved a rapprochement that is healthy for both. Many of the top "name" performers in the early music field today profess themselves just as interested and just as comfortable working on more modern works with mainstream orchestras. This seems to me to be an utterly healthy, rational and laudable development.

To return, for the sake of an example, to the subject of the Mozart piano concertos: why cannot audiences have it both ways? Why do we have to necessarily jettison the one in order to have the other? These are works that speak to us just as vitally from a nine-foot Steinway as they do from the most carefully reconstructed Mozart-era fortepiano. Why do we have to forego hearing our great modern orchestras play the Brandenburg Concertos just because there are those who prefer them on "original instruments?"

I think that common sense and rationality have prevailed. No one questions the invaluable contributions made to musical life over the past 50 years by the early music movement; these ideas constitute a true revelation. But that does not mean that we sweep the field clear of any and all other interpretive approaches. Each age, after all, reinterprets these great works in its own way, just as great works of literature or theater (think Shakespeare!) are reinterpreted long after the literary or theatrical conventions of their own day have passed from the scene. We can, in the words of the old cliché, have our cake and eat it too.

I think from the point of view of the mainstream concertgoer — especially he/she who is just beginning to find classical music attractive — it is a good idea to approach early music gradually, at one's own speed and without force-feeding it. You do have to retune your ears and your historical-musical calendar fairly drastically to enter that world. You cannot listen to Machaut the same way you listen to La Boheme. This is a message from a vanished time and place, but just because it is old and perhaps a little strange-sounding at first, that does not mean it is not just as valuable. Fifty years ago even the opportunity to get to know this music was severely restricted. People who professed a serious interest in it were, first of all, few and far between; secondly, they were looked at by their friends from the mainstream symphony audience as perhaps a little tetched in the head. No longer. A whole new library of great music has been made known to the world. Something truly wonderful has happened.

III. WOLFGANG AMADEUS MOZART
(1756-1791)

Let's start with a simple statement of fact: Wolfgang Amadeus Mozart was the greatest natural-born musical genius who has ever walked the earth.

Consider that here was a man who produced whole strings of masterworks in every genre of concert music, from the simple song to opera, symphony and concerto, and who seemed to do it almost effortlessly. The testimony of his contemporaries is full of stories about Mozart enjoying a convivial evening with friends, but every now and then stepping aside to note down some musical idea that had occurred to him. He loved to play billiards (one item in his rather meager estate when he died at not-quite-36 was a billiard table), and there are authentic stories about his seeming ability to play billiards and compose music more or less at the same time.

He was also, of course, a child prodigy as both composer and performer, and into his short life he packed enough touring, performing and composing for three or four normal mortals. The register of his works compiled by the music-loving lawyer Ludwig Köchel runs up to number 626, starting with three little keyboard minuets (K. 1) and ending with the unfinished Requiem.

Not all of this music, of course, is of equal quality, but the percentage of authentic recognized masterworks in it is astoundingly high, and a very respectable total of those 626 works remain in the active repertory today.

Some years ago, the orchestra in my home city undertook over several seasons the presentation of all 41 of Mozart's generally recognized symphonies, of which eight or ten are fixtures in the standard repertory. The first 20 or so of these works (considered chronologically) are not especially remarkable when assessed in a kind of musical vacuum. As the pieces were performed one by one, one heard arresting details and felicitous touches throughout, but these early works proved more naively charming than anything else, until you reminded yourself that this music was the work of a child — a 7 or 8-year-old in the case of the earliest pieces, a teenager for some of the later ones. This realization changed everything; a pleasant musical diversion suddenly turned into a miracle. The experience created a valuable and seldom-appreciated context for the incontestably greater symphonies that begin roughly with the early G minor work, no. 25 (K. 183), written when Mozart was 17.

Mozart was taken in hand by his father when still a small child and set to touring around Europe as a prodigy, performing for royalty and nobility and anyone else whom the ambitious Leopold Mozart felt might bestow money and fame upon his remarkable son. Father and son carried on a quite remarkable love-hate relationship for many years after that, even long after Wolfgang had begun to make his way in the world on his own.

Leopold did not quite understand the incredible things that were happening inside his son's brain; he kept admonishing Wolfgang not to disdain doing the popular thing, urged him to curry favor with influential people, and to write music that had wide popular appeal. Wolfgang put up with this hectoring to a certain extent, but he made clear to his father that his artistic aim was to do things better than anyone else had done them. And he did.

Two primary examples — the two fields in which Mozart perhaps made the greatest of all his musical contributions — were the piano concerto and the opera.

When Mozart took up the piano concerto as a teenager, it was a form in its artistic infancy, scarcely developed beyond the idea of the piano as a kind of first-among-equals in the instrumental ensemble. Starting from this unpromising base, and motivated largely by his wish to provide himself with vehicles for his own concert appearances, and, in a number of later cases, to provide vehicles for his pupils, Mozart created an incomparable series of masterpieces, utterly transforming the pedestrian form of his predecessors and, for all practical purposes, inventing the piano concerto as we still know it today.

There are about 27 of these pieces, depending on how you count the first two or three, which are actually transcriptions of music by other composers.

The first of his incontestable masterworks in this form is the remarkable E flat concerto, K. 271, written for a French virtuoso, Mlle. Jeunehomme (we do not even know her first name), who passed through Mozart's home town of Salzburg. Mozart wrote this extraordinary piece at the age of 21. He flouted tradition in several ways; first by introducing the soloist (for a single phrase) at the very outset instead of waiting out the traditional orchestral exposition; second by what my ears at least perceive as the unusual depth and seriousness of the slow movement; and third by inserting in the middle of his rondo finale a ravishing miniature theme and variations episode in slow tempo.

The wondrous succession of great piano concerti that followed (there were six of them in the year 1784 alone) epitomizes all that is advanced, civilized and beautiful in Mozart's music as a whole. There is, for example, a superbly maintained equality of balance between piano and orchestra in all these pieces. These concertos are not duels between two antagonists like the concertos Brahms was to write; nor are they exquisite piano solo vehicles set against an often perfunctory orchestral backdrop, like those of Chopin. They are intricate and civilized conversations between piano and orchestra, each one somehow incomplete without the complementary interplay of the other.

Time after time, in these concertos the cool objective eye of the score-reader will note that the orchestral part is nothing especially original or striking, and that the piano part that goes with it is fairly formulaic and decorative, but when the two are put together, something emerges that is somehow much more than the sum of those two parts. Other composers of Mozart's time tried to bring off this mysterious alchemy, but none succeeded so brilliantly or so consistently as did Mozart.

These concertos are not particularly "difficult" in the conventional Liszt-Rachmaninoff sense of great clumps of notes sprayed out at high speed and overpowering volume. Their problems rather concern style, phrasing, purity of line and sympathetic rapport with the orchestra. They are not "showy" enough for some pianists (and some audiences). But they mark one of the great peaks of human artistic achievement.

The same considerations apply in many ways to Mozart's operas (there are 20 or so of them, depending again on how you classify some of his very youthful efforts). The classic operatic form of his day was the opera seria, a serious piece, usually on a mythological or royal subject, with stock characters and situations, much scenic display and a full complement of da capo arias, in which the action stood still for several minutes while a character expressed his emotional state in highly decorative music that followed a rigid A-B-A formal scheme, with the second "A" section being an ornamented repeat of the first (hence the designation da capo — "from the beginning".)

Mozart brought opera seria to a peak of dramatic expressiveness in Idomeneo, premiered when he was 25 and still performed today, though not nearly so often as it merits. Meanwhile, however, he had created an entirely new form of opera, one which mingled comic and serious elements, presented clearly-drawn complex characters in believable situations and endowed them with arias and ensembles that served to advance the action rather than to bring it to a halt. The opera, like the piano concerto, was a wholly different artistic entity when Mozart got through dealing with it. Both genres had been forever transformed by his genius. With the exception of the relatively early Entfuhrung aus dem Serail (Abuction from the Seraglio), none of these major innovative late Mozart operas is quite what it seems on the surface. Le Nozze di Figaro (The Marriage of Figaro), based on a subversive French play, is a sardonic commentary on class distinctions and the uneasy relationship of masters and servants in a world where the servants were beginning to assert their rights; Don Giovanni is a kind of moral allegory of good and evil, but is also not without its own commentary on social classes, as witness the relationship of the Don to his servant, and the various social classes represented by the three women involved with the Don. Die Zauberflote (The Magic Flute) is a complex Masonic-religious allegory whose precise meaning is debated by scholars to this very day. Even the most innocent-seeming of all these wonderful operas, Cosi fan Tutte (All Women are Like That) carries an underlying vein of sardonic commentary about the eternal battle of the sexes. There is still debate today, for example, over whether at the final curtain of this ostensible lightweight comedy, the two pairs of lovers return to their original lineup, or whether the rearrangement affected by the outwardly farcical plot is preserved (a perceptive friend of mine has remarked that the couples should remain in their new alignment, because if they returned to the status quo ante their relationships would be forever poisoned by doubt and suspicions of inconstancy).

Yet two of these operas, Figaro and Cosi, can be viewed on the surface as "just" comedies. Don Giovanni and Zauberflote have plenty of comic content, but both are obviously more than comedies (Mozart enigmatically dubbed Don Giovanni a dramma giocosa on its title page, thus leaving the comic-tragic question hanging in ambiguity).

All of this would be of mainly sociological interest, however, were it not for the miracle of Mozart's music, which is intricate and sophisticated in the highest degree, while always remaining beautiful and expressive too. Over the years, for example, there has been much debate over what many have deemed the flimsy and indeed silly libretto of Cosi fan Tutte. (Beethoven, who had a prudish side, considered it immoral). The opera went through a long period of neglect by an opera world that tried hard to explain away the libretto but seems seldom to have listened to the music with which Mozart clothed it.

A major virtue of these operas is the same sort of intricate yet perfect balance between diverse elements that we find in the piano concertos. Voices and orchestra are somehow welded into a single organism, neither one quite complete without the other. That which sounds simple, even inevitable, turns out upon closer examination to be made up of the most intricate sort of detail. One characteristic of the greatest art is its ability to hide its own complexity from public view; it makes highly intricate things look (or sound) easy. Mozart's music — orchestral, operatic, chamber music, solo pieces, the whole lot — accomplishes this magical feat consistently and well.

Mozart and Beethoven have one thing in common: a consuming interest in their private lives on the part of the general public today. Mozart's life was interesting, first of all because it was so short, and he was able to accomplish so much during it; secondly, the child prodigy has always been a figure of some interest to the general public, and Mozart was surely the most remarkable musical prodigy who has ever lived; thirdly, Mozart achieved a good deal of success and honor in his life, but never made much money (or at least was never able to hold on to much of the money he did make), and the fact that his life was mostly a struggle against want has helped to romanticize him.

Mozart summed up the Classical era in music,

brought it to a pitch of unrivaled perfection, and even, here and there in his later works, began moving it toward the dawning Romantic era. In particular one might cite the dark-tinted D minor piano concerto (K. 466), the late G minor symphony (K. 550) and the elementally powerful final scene of Don Giovanni as Mozartean homage to the dawn of Romanticism in music.

It is a mistake, as it is with most composers, to restrict ones gaze only to their major works in the glamorous large-scale forms. Mozart wrote so much music in all forms that it is possible to find worthwhile pieces in all of them, though of course more consistently in some than in others. I do not feel, for example, that Mozart's contribution to the piano sonata literature, though certainly considerable, matches in consistent quality what he did in concerto, symphony and opera; yet there are some truly beautiful things — complete works as well as individual movements — scattered through those 19 or so sonatas.

He also wrote a number of really lovely concert songs (not to be confused with the concert arias written for interpolation in works by other composers); a personal favorite of mine is the exquisite Abendempfindung (Evening Mood), K. 523. Among Mozart's religious music that is less often heard, I can recommend the superb Vesprae Solennes de Confessore, K. 339. The gems scattered through Mozart's catalogue of chamber music are simply too numerous to mention short of providing a wearisome list of titles and Köchel numbers.

Is there any rational explanation for the emergence of Wolfgang Amadeus Mozart? True, his father was a fine musician in his own right, but that, and more, can be said of a good many fine composers. A lot of dazzling prodigies have come along over the course of musical history, and many of them have achieved great things, but there is still only one Mozart. What wild concatenation of circumstances, genes, environment, will, or whatever, was at work here, and can we ever expect such a thing again?

I think there is no answer to such cosmic questions. What there is, however, is food for thought. The finger of God, or whatever you may wish to call it, somehow touched Mozart. Whether you are of religious inclination or not, it seems to me obvious that there is something at work here beyond human ken or understanding. I think of him as having received a Divine Spark, though exactly how such things happen I have not the foggiest idea. At this level of art it seems to me we approach the boundaries of the supernatural.

However you may view this idea, it seems indisputable that Mozart represents our consistent musical best when you take into account the breadth of his achievement and the short lifetime into which it was compressed.

If Mozart had lived as long as Beethoven did, he would have heard and known the early operas of Rossini, all the Beethoven symphonies except the ninth, some of Weber's works and maybe even some of the teenaged

Schubert. To imagine what he might have written in those extra years boggles the mind. Conversely, if Beethoven had died as young as Mozart did we would have today only the first three of his symphonies, and we would lack all the late piano sonatas, the violin concerto, Egmont, the Missa Solemnis, all the late string quartets and the final version of Fidelio. As for Bach, had he died as young as Mozart we would possess today none of his great choral works and there would be no Brandenburg Concertos.

None of this is meant to disparage other great composers, of course. Choosing "the greatest" in any field is little more than a parlor game. I merely point out the extraordinarily brief span of years granted to Mozart in which to make his mark, and the astounding diversity of musical genres in which he made that mark brilliantly — not once or twice, but many times over. Even his "occasional" pieces, tossed off quickly for specific occasions or performers, often bear the stamp of exquisite balance, perfection of detail and superb overall workmanship that are his hallmarks. They may not be great music, but they bear the unmistakable stamp of the genius that created them.

IV. JOHANNES BRAHMS (1833-1897)

Here we encounter a curious case among composers now universally considered great. Like so many other composers, Brahms went through his Purgatorial Period of being considered "controversial," but in his case it was for reasons quite different from the usual, and even in some measure irrelevant to his music itself.

In mid-career Brahms found himself willy-nilly set up as a stylistic counterweight to Wagner. Wagner was wildly controversial during his lifetime, and remained so for several generations after his death. You were either a member of the Wagner cult or its enemy, and the opposition for some reason began coalescing around the music of Brahms as its chosen alternative. Brahms never encouraged this, and indeed expressed great respect for Wagner; but the movements and machinations of musical politics, then as now, had a life of their own.

It is important — and quite difficult at this late date — for us to remember too that Brahms was not controversial because he was avant-garde. He was rather regarded as old-fashioned, backward looking, dull and pedantic. It was not all that long ago, as history is measured, that the great Boston music critic Philip Hale suggested only half-jokingly that the exit doors in Symphony Hall in that city be labeled "exits in case of Brahms."

This dismissal as old hat was a fate that Brahms shared posthumously with Bach, one of whose sons reportedly referred to his father as an "old peruke." Not bad company for Brahms to keep, whatever the reason.

Brahms is today solidly established in the musical mainstream. His four symphonies are heard with a frequency comparable to those of Beethoven; his two massive piano concertos, his lovely lyrical violin concerto and his brilliant double concerto for violin, cello and orchestra are staples of the repertory. The German Requiem is sung by choruses everywhere; pianists regularly offer his technically difficult but rewarding piano music and singers program his lovely songs.

There is a prevailing serious tone to most of his music that goes along with the reports we have of his personality. He could be gruff to bothersome strangers, and they say one had to get to know him well to see his genial side. There are a number of stories extant of his unwillingness to suffer fools gladly. He never married, though there is general agreement that he fell in love with Clara Schumann and would have liked to marry her after his friend Robert Schumann died. Of all the great composers, Brahms is probably the least known in any personal sense to the general public. Mozart, Beethoven, Wagner, Bach, Schubert, Tchaikovsky all have quite well-defined human "personalities" in the public mind, but Brahms remains pretty much just the name of someone who happened to write some of the world's most beautiful music.

Brahms was an agnostic, yet he wrote one of the most philosophically beautiful of requiems, and he set to music many a text with overt or secondary religious implications. He seems to have believed in the existence of God, but if he had any formal religious convictions at all he kept them completely to himself. His great German Requiem is an entirely personal and idiosyncratic construction that has nothing in common with the Latin text of the formal churchly requiem.

This side of his nature has given rise to one of the more intriguing minor mysteries of music: In 1955 there appeared a curious book, Talks With Great Composers, in which writer Arthur M. Abell claimed to be reporting the substance of a long conversation in 1896 involving himself, Brahms and the violinist Joseph Joachim. In this encounter, Brahms described the mental state into which he entered when composing, terming it one of "divine inspiration." He talks at length and in detail about his Christian faith, with copious quotes from the Bible to illustrate his points.

The Philosophical Library reprinted this book in 1987. I had never heard of it or of its author, and I was frankly astonished at the idea of Brahms as a believing Christian. It goes against everything one can read about the man in biographies and contemporary memoirs. I have a letter on the subject from a pre-eminent Brahms scholar (who has since died) in which he terms the whole thing "pure fiction." Abell is long since dead too, so there is really no way to arrive at the truth of this interview which may or may not have happened a century ago between a great composer (who was to die four months after the purported conversation) and a then-young American music student. But Abell's book remains available to keep the debate boiling.

There is a lighter vein to the music of Brahms, but it is not large and you have to search a little to find it. For me, it comes out most engagingly in the two sets of Liebeslieder (Love-song) waltzes for piano duet and vocal quartet. These are delightfully gemuetlich pieces that glide along on a tide of Germanic sentimental nostalgia. Of the four symphonies, only the fourth has a true scherzo movement, and even that piece sounds to me more like exuberant horseplay than true humor. In most of the rest of his output, Brahms seldom goes beyond a kind of gentle geniality or, in the finales of major works, an air of extroverted symphonic brilliance appropriate to the occasion. The delightful Academic Festival Overture, constructed on German student songs, is full of sturdy undergraduate good cheer.

The little set of waltzes for piano, op. 39, also bespeaks a more genial Brahms. But beyond these few pieces most of his output bears a generally serious tone. It is certainly full of passion and highly charged emotion, but there is always a controlling discipline there, a sense that things will never go off the emotional rails because an overarching musical intelligence is firmly in command. There is a wonderful example of this in the finale of the great D minor piano concerto where the piano falls silent for a minute or so, while the orchestra engages in a superb miniature contrapuntal episode (a little fugato) based loosely on one of the subsidiary themes of the movement. It is all over in less than a minute, but it is music of quicksilver elegance and polish, as if Brahms were saying to us "You see, fellow, there is more than one way to have a good time at this game!"

Brahms' life was comparatively tranquil, lacking the melodramatics that dogged Tchaikovsky, Wagner and Beethoven or the constant threat of poverty that hung over Mozart. His music can therefore in the main be considered by and for itself, without obvious reference to external events. This may have been one reason why it took him a relatively long time to reach the status of an unchallenged classic master, for the public loves these extramusical associations that it can hang onto pieces of music like moustaches on the Mona Lisa; it has a harder time coming to terms with someone who simply says, "Here is my music — how do you like it?" It is always easier, and almost invariably more misleading, to deal with music in dramatic or extra-musical terms than in terms of itself.

The mistake made by those anti-Brahmsian Boston concertgoers noted by Philip Hale (and by their cohorts in other places) was to confuse Brahms' admittedly sober, serious musical personality with simple dullness. In artistic matters, sobriety and dullness may be kissing cousins, but they are not blood brothers. The one does not necessarily entail the other, as Bach, for one, proved virtually every time he put pen to score paper.

Brahms is never dull. His music encompasses a wide range of human emotions, from the great ocean-roll of the first movement of the first symphony to the spiritual exaltation of the Requiem and the warmth of much of his piano music, but he is never a bore. Perhaps his greatest claim to immortality, in fact, may lie exactly in this skillful blending of technique with emotional content; it is all done in such a way that the technical mastery is all but invisible. It is there, underlying everything, giving the music shape, backbone and logical coherence, but it almost never calls attention to itself.

This is almost a textbook definition of great art. When we stand awestruck before some famous cathedral — Chartres, Cologne, Westminster — we are transported by the sight of a great, soaring building. The stonework seems to lift our own minds up toward heaven even as it lifts itself; but hidden behind that vision there lie careful calculations — plans, drawings, stress calculations, mathematical formulas, an unseen utilitarian framework that holds the whole thing together and allows to it sing to our spirit. We never give any of this a thought (unless we are ourselves architects), but it is there, and without it there could be no cathedral. The same principle applies to great works of art.

This was Brahms' way of working. Perhaps the best and most famous example of this in his output is the finale of his fourth symphony, an entire movement built on variations of the simple eight-note theme announced by the brass at the outset. Sometimes the theme is heard backwards, sometimes it is artfully hidden in the rhythmic accompaniment. Sometimes it is utterly obvious to even the least attentive listener; sometimes it is so unobtrusive that you cannot tell it's there without studying the score. But it is always there somewhere. Brahms plays a game of learned hide-and-seek with us as we listen. Like Walt Whitman, he teases us:

> Failing to fetch me at first, keep encouraged.
> Missing me one place search another,
> I stop somewhere waiting for you.

This sort of thing, of course, is the common coin of all variation-pieces; but in this movement Brahms has done the trick not with a whole melody, but with a mere succession of eight notes, a motif rather than a melody. Even if somehow you manage to pay no heed to the variation technique employed in this powerful music, it can still make a wonderful effect purely through its potency as music. The underpinning of technical mastery is simply there, working its magic unobserved.

Brahms also stands apart from many of the great composers by the fact that he made such important contributions in the fields of chamber music and other smaller forms, in addition to working in the high-visibility fields of symphony and concerto. If you know only the choral-orchestral Brahms you are missing something very important. He wrote two magnificent string sextets, for example, which are almost never heard in live performance, perhaps simply because not that many concerts involving string sextets are ever given. There are three superb piano quartets and a piano quintet, a trio for piano, violin and horn, a clarinet quintet, three string quartets and a number of other works. There is even a set of lovely sonatas (op. 120) that can be played by either clarinet or viola (they also sound just fine on the violin).

Among his less familiar orchestral works, I would like to plead the case of the two early serenades, opp. 11 and 16, the second of them dispensing with violins in its orchestra. There are several short works for chorus and orchestra, the famous Alto Rhapsody and Schicksalslied (Song of Fate), and the lesser-known Nanie, and Gesang der Parzen (Song of Fate).

The famous Vier Ernste Gesange (Four Serious Songs), and the two op. 91 songs for voice, viola and piano are only the beginning of Brahms' extensive list of beautiful songs. From the long list, I select just two personal favorites: Wie Melodien Zieht es Mir (As Melodies a feeling steals through me),op. 105, no. 1, and

Wie bist du, Meine Konigin (How Blissful, my Queen)
from the op. 20 group of vocal duets. The piano parts of
Brahms's songs are complicated and technically difficult;
any performance of them calls for a true collaboration of
equal partners, not for a simplistic soloist/accompanist
arrangement.

Brahms was himself an excellent pianist. He produced the two massive and justly famous piano concertos
that are today in the front rank of popularity, and also a
large body of beautiful solo music that turns up regularly
on recital programs. The rhapsodies, intermezzi, capric-
cios and other works that make up his opp. 76 and 116-119
are well worth knowing. There is a caution to be made
here, though: Brahms thought of the piano in orchestral
terms. His piano writing tends to be thickly chorded and
intricate. It takes a really sympathetic (and competent)
player to master this complex style and make it sound
natural. The rewards — for player as well as listener —
are very great indeed, but they do not come easy.

Among the Brahms sonatas there are three for piano
solo and several others for cello and violin with piano.
A particular gem is the lovely violin sonata in D minor,
op. 108.

Brahms never wrote an opera, though the evidence
of his music suggests that he might have done so successfully. There is drama there aplenty, but it is drama
expressed in purely abstract terms, within the boundaries
of the musical conventions of his day. The two piano
concertos have often and quite justly been described

as dramatic encounters, even battles for supremacy, between piano and orchestra; and the evidence of his many songs and considerable body of choral music shows that he was one of the great masters of writing for the voice.

Brahms was a composer content to work in established forms and within the then-currently accepted harmonic framework of music. Only perhaps in the large dimensions and symphonic style of his two big piano concertos and in the idiosyncratic form of his nonliturgical German Requiem did he try to go beyond those norms, and in both cases the results were triumphant.

Not everyone in the arts is cut out to be an innovator. Brahms did not complete his first symphony until he was well into his forties, claiming that the burden of coming after Beethoven was an almost fatal inhibiting factor for any newcomer to the symphonic lists. But when he did produce that superb symphony, it was instantly recognized as a masterwork in its own right.

Brahms was content to be himself; that may have contributed to the delay in his acceptance as a master composer. A perceptive comment that sums him up about as well as any came from the vastly influential Viennese critic Eduard Hanslick, remembered mostly today as an inveterate foe of Wagner. Hanslick admired much of Brahms's music and had great respect for him; but when he attended the premiere of the fourth symphony he was puzzled and disappointed. The music seemed to him cold and unemotional despite its obvious technical brilliance. His review was detailed and eminently fair, though basically disapproving. He ended with this splendid sentence: "It is like a dark well; the longer we look into it, the more brightly the stars shine back."

V. FRANZ SCHUBERT (1797-1828)

Look again, reader, at those dates of birth and death. We deal here with the shortest-lived of all the indisputably great composers. Schubert's life was about five years shorter than Mozart's; his genius lacked the range of Mozart's, but in its chosen musical fields it worked wonders.

Schubert excelled in the art song, in chamber music and in music for solo piano. He wrote nine symphonies, all of them estimable and three of them admissible into the ranks of true masterpieces. On the other hand, he wrote no instrumental concertos, and none of his six operas have left more than faint traces behind.

Confronting again the sticky question of the influence of a composer's personal affairs on (a) his music and (b) his posthumous reputation, we find in Schubert a peculiar case. In objective terms, Schubert did not lead a happy life; he was dogged by want through all his 31 short years — yet much of his music radiates pure joy, or at least an optimistic outlook. This fact seems to reflect the sunny nature of his personality, a characteristic confirmed by the testimony of many who knew him. As to his posthumous reputation, there has been a fair amount of hand wringing over his early death, and back in the 1920s his music was even ransacked to make a saccharine Broadway opus called Blossom Time. Lately, however, concern with his private life has taken a more contemporary turn: we used to read that he died of venereal disease; now we read that he may have been the center of a homosexual circle in Vienna.

I personally find all of this irrelevant, preferring simply to hear the music and be transported by it. It is not a case like that of Tchaikovsky, in which the composer's private life is indisputably reflected in his music. In my view the supposed reflections of Schubert's private life appear to have been projected back into the music by researchers who wanted very much to find them there.

It was also said of Schubert that the defects in his music — defects gleefully pointed out for generations by musicologists and just as gleefully ignored by the listening public — were the result of sketchy formal musical training. Only in reaction to that sort of nitpicking has the realization dawned that these "defects" may have simply been the way a genius chose to work. They may have been Schubert going about the business of being Schubert, which should be quite enough for those who want to listen.

Schubert is longwinded, they say. His idea of symphonic development is to take a theme and repeat it verbatim in two or three quite alien keys before turning back on himself and restating it again in the home key. And his famously abrupt shifts from key to key still puzzle the analysts, while simultaneously delighting the listener.

This is a variation on the often-cited theme of the genius who makes up his own rules. Moussorgsky, a composer who was indisputably poorly trained (and who also died very young) suffered for many years from this same idea that his music was disorganized and chaotic. Unfortunately for him, he had at his elbow a coterie of better-educated academics who, with all good intentions, took his scores and refashioned them more in conformity with academic orthodoxy, thereby planing away much of their individuality. Only in recent years have we been persuaded to go back to Moussorgsky's originals and have found to our surprise and delight that the man knew exactly what he was doing. As Charles Ives once wrote in a note to his score-copyist: "Mr. Price: Don't change anything. All the wrong notes are right."

Without that leisurely pace, without those unconventional key-shifts, Schubert would simply not be Schubert. His music would still be eminently worth hearing, but a lot of what makes it truly great would be missing. Robert Schumann spoke perhaps even truer than he knew when he delivered his famous salute to the "heavenly length" of the "Great" C major symphony (formerly listed as no. 7, now known as no. 9).

Schubert's gregarious habits and innate good nature made him the center of a convivial group of musicians in Vienna that used to meet in coffeehouses and private homes for informal evenings of music making — the so-called "Schubertiads." His latest lied, piano piece or work of chamber music would be tried out for a circle of admirers. Schubert, who seemed unconcerned with the fate of his pieces, would often give his manuscripts to friends as souvenirs of such an ephemeral occasion, or stow them away someplace afterwards and forget about them. This has been the despair of musicologists ever since and has led to the curious fact that, practically to this day, previously unknown pieces reputed to be Schubert's keep turning up in dusty libraries, moldy attics and the recesses of obscure castles. His two best-known symphonies — the two works by which he is best known to symphonic audiences today — were not discovered until after his death. The story of the discovery of the Unfinished Symphony's manuscript in a dusty old trunk in 1865, 37 years after its composer's death, is famous. The "Great" C major symphony had a single performance shortly after Schubert's death, but then lay forgotten for a decade or more until it was rediscovered by Robert Schumann.

But it is indisputably in the field of the German lied (art song, as opposed to folksong) that Schubert made musical history. Careful counters have concluded that there are 634 of them from his pen. They constitute a treasure which is all the more of a treasure because it is virtually unknown to a sizable segment of the music-loving public. A number of other composers — Brahms, Schumann, Mahler, Wolf, Richard Strauss — contributed notably to this genre, but Franz Schubert, for all practical purposes, invented it, and brought it to a peak of consistent perfection unmatched by the others.

These songs come in all musical shapes and sizes. There are extended scenas like Der Hirt auf dem Felsen (The Shepherd on the Rock), pieces that sound like quaint folk songs, like Heidenroslein (Hedge-Roses), powerful miniature dramas like Der Doppelganger (The Double) and sheer lyrical effusions like Auf dem Wasser zu Singen (To Be Sung on the Water). There are narratives and simple expressions of uncomplicated emotions; there are love-songs and war-songs, grim songs about death and humorous ditties.

The list includes two great song-cycle dramas, Die Schoene Mullerin (The Beautiful Mill-Girl) and Die Winterreise (Winter-Journey) which can grip us in performance fully as much as does any elaborate opera with full orchestra and a "cast of thousands."

I mentioned earlier that none of Schubert's six operas has survived on the stage. In more than half a century of enthusiastic opera going, I have witnessed just one single performance of a Schubert opera. It was Fierabras, in which Schubert's music was shackled to a truly absurd libretto. The individual pieces were indeed lovely, but they left the impression of a string of lieder hung on the text like clothes on a washing-line. There was little in the score of the kind of dramatic tension that one associates with the world of opera. Schubert achieved that tension, time and again, within the bounds of a single three-minute song, but it eluded him over the span of a whole evening.

Die Schoene Mullerin and Winterreise are Schubert's real operas, and they are incredibly gripping masterpieces, holding the listener bound by their power for an entire evening through the modest medium of a single singer and a pianist. Scenery, costumes, drama are left to the imagination of the listener, stirred and prompted by Schubert's music and the words of the poets. They are there in the mind's eye as surely as they would be at any elaborately staged Aida or Turandot.

The great classic example of this in Schubert's song output is of course the incomparable Erl-King, a macabre ghost story that runs its tragic course in three or four minutes. The singer is required in this justly famous song to have four distinct voices — the impersonal narrator who sets the scene at the beginning and brings down the curtain with tragic abruptness at the end; the anxious father; the sick child; and the seductive voice of the malevolent Erl-King himself. The pianist, dealing with that famously exhausting piano part, is himself almost a fifth character in the drama.

I recall once hearing a masterly performance of this song at a recital by Dietrich Fischer-Dieskau and feeling that it might well be considered a whole concert by itself. I could conceive of arriving at a hall some day, hearing such a superb performance of this song - and then leaving, fully satisfied that I had taken on enough musical, poetic, emotional and philosophical nourishment to sustain me for the whole evening. There would be no question of asking for money back at the box office.

Quite at the opposite extreme from this dark drama is another song of an utterly different cast — Auf dem Wasser zu Singen, as pure a lyrical flight as there is in all music. The words to this song, by one Friedrich Leopold Graf zu Stolberg, are vague and untranslatable from the German into any sort of sensible English; they deal in high-flown poetic terms with the transitoriness of human existence. But in reality, this is a case where the meaning of the words is simply unimportant. Schubert has clothed Stolberg's verse in such a ravishing flowing melody and such a rippling piano accompaniment (perhaps suggested by the water-imagery of title and poem) that nothing more is needed. I know that knowledge of the words is a vital element in the listener's appreciation of virtually all art songs, but I submit this piece as the exception that proves the rule. A further curious fact about this wonderful song is that the piano part, if performed entirely independently of the vocal line, makes a splendid technical study for independence of the fingers of the right hand.

Schubert's strongest point in everything he produced

is his melodic fecundity. His music is full of tunes that, once heard, twine themselves around brain and memory forever. His detractors even bring up this very facility as a point against him. All very well, they harrumph, to have all those lovely themes floating around in your music, but you have to be able to develop them, to do something with them, in order to call yourself a real composer. This seems to me a shortsighted view, to put things charitably. Schubert was quite capable of writing symphonic developments of the traditional sort when he wanted to, and doing it very well (e.g., the first movement of the Unfinished Symphony, a development section based almost exclusively not on the movement's main theme but on its introduction), but in many a memorable case he simply chose to do things his own way.

This is evident in many of the piano sonatas, a genre in which I feel Schubert's contribution is often undervalued. He has a habit of suddenly swerving off from the principal key and bringing his music, almost without warning, not into a harmonically related key but into one that is quite remote. It is at once a Schubertian personal fingerprint and an integral part of the music's charm.

Schubert's piano music in general does not strike me (an amateur devotee of it) as especially "pianistic." Some of its figurations lie awkwardly under the fingers and there are wide skips that can give the unwary pianist all kinds of trouble. But the impulse toward instrumental song is there in every bar, and all of this music is well worth toiling over. The last three great pianos sonatas (C minor, A major and B-flat major) are justly famous for their broad scope and philosophical depth, but there are a number of others that pianists should pay more attention to — e.g., the earlier and smaller one in A major (Op. 120).

Schubert's chamber music — 15 string quartets, several string and piano trios, a clutch of lovely pieces for violin and piano, the great C major string quintet and the famous Octet — partakes, like much of his best music, of the characteristics of the lied. Many of these pieces are in some sense extended lieder, and several of them, of course, are actually based on his songs (the famous Trout quintet, the Death and the Maiden quartet, the Wanderer fantasy for piano solo). The same impulse toward "singing on instruments" is evident throughout Schubert's substantial output of shorter piano pieces; the two beautiful sets of impromptus (opp. 90 and 142) are but one example among a large and varied output.

Schubert also made a notable contribution to the much-neglected genre of music for male chorus. Indeed, he produced so much music that one can stumble upon unexpected joys in many an odd neglected corner of his output. With him, even more than with other great composers, it is a mistake to confine oneself to the well publicized and the often performed. Performers willing to shine their lamps into the lesser-known recesses of his large output are valuable fellows indeed, and should be encouraged.

Schubert's melodies often have a sense of inevitability about them, as though they had just dropped down from Heaven and were simply waiting for the first composer to come along, notice them, pick them up and give them voice. Such, to my ears, among many examples, are the lovely flowing second theme in the opening movement of the great C Major String Quintet, op. 165, and the almost waltz-like Et Incarnatus Est of the great Mass in E flat. Schubert's masses (there are six of them) are regarded as liturgically inadmissible by the church, I am told, because he takes liberties with the Latin text; but they are ravishingly beautiful works that choruses in general would be well advised to program more often.

Schubert is often painted as a kind of overgrown musical child, an artless, guileless singer who just kept pouring out beautiful music without any consciousness of his own powers. This view seems to me incompatible with the passages in his works that betray incredible emotional depths, especially in a song like Der Doppelganger, or quintessentially in one like the bleak Der Leiermann (The Organ-Grinder), the final song in Winterreise.

Considered simply as notes on paper, Der Leiermann is among the simplest pieces of music ever written. A bare open-fifth drone is sounded 63 times by the pianist's left hand; the voice part tells its melancholy tale of insanity and obsession in a few pale phrases of recitative, and the pianist's right hand delivers a series of simple figures that suggest — but do not paint literally — the music of the hand-organ. Everything is uniformly soft. The music does not so much end as does it simply stop, exhausted. This is the end of the mournful song-story; the nameless hero drifts offstage, a wandering madman. There is no eloquent epilogue from the piano, just that eternal open fifth droning away. Schubert gives us no final transfiguring note of pity or catharsis.

I know of no great extended work of music that ends so bleakly, with music less calculated to bring bravos, cheers and bouquets of flowers. Is this "beautiful" music in the commonly accepted sense? I think not. It is music meant to convey a truth. The man who wrote it cannot have been an uncomplicated fellow, a man like the rest of us. There are things that art can do that are more important than simply being beautiful.

VI. FELIX MENDELSSOHN (1809-1847)

We deal here with something very uncommon in the history of music — a career that was wildly successful from the very start and a composer whose life, though tragically short, was happy and fulfilling. Mendelssohn came from a wealthy family, traveled widely, married happily and was universally celebrated. He never had to worry about money and his personal life seems to have been unblemished.

His first name, of course, means "happy" in Latin. I remarked earlier that comfortable circumstances seldom seem to produce great works of music. Mendelssohn, a composer whose music is consistently undervalued these days, may be a shining exception to that rule. Some day, one hopes, his reputation may be reassessed and substantially upgraded.

Mendelssohn was also a child prodigy almost on a par with Mozart. He appeared in public as a pianist at 9, and wrote two of his best and most famous instrumental works while still a teenager, the brilliant Octet and the famous Midsummer Night's Dream Overture. His music's great virtues are elegance, refinement, civilized good taste and brilliance. True, it does not in general run very deep, but it remains tuneful, expertly crafted, pleasure-giving and — need one add? — popular.

Hard-pressed music critics have a habit of turning the names of composers into adjectives. We know exactly what is meant when a piece is described as "Beethovenian," "Puccinian" or "Wagnerian." The term "Mendelssohnian" describes music that is fleet-footed, light-textured, perhaps ephemeral, but nonetheless totally charming. It refers back to pieces like the Midsummer Night's Dream scherzo, the finale of Mendelssohn's D minor trio or any number of his fairy-music piano pieces, e.g. the famous little E minor scherzo that has bedeviled many a piano student. Not a bad way to be remembered.

One place where Hamburg-born Mendelssohn was extremely popular was England. He made ten trips there, was wildly feted everywhere and conducted there the world premiere of his most ambitious work, the Biblical oratorio Elijah. In a strange way this English popularity has reacted against his reputation, for his name became linked with the manners and spirit of the much-maligned (after the fact) Victorian era. (George Bernard Shaw characteristically sneered that Mendelssohn was the world's greatest composer to all those who also thought Tennyson the world's greatest poet). This lent to Mendelssohn's name the aura of one who wrote perfumed trifles for proper young ladies to toy with, and genteel concert pieces that stuffy people could listen to without disturbing their preoccupation with matters more important than mere art. This was an injustice to Mendelssohn; he may not have spoken with Beethovenian thunders, but his music has virtues that go far beyond the prim and the genteel. And the historians are now telling us that the Victorians were nowhere near so prim and genteel as they have been painted. Charles Dickens, born just three years after Mendelssohn, is dismissed by some (mostly by people who have not read him) today as a mere "Victorian" novelist not worth reading any more; but he was in reality as trenchant (and effective) a social critic as ever put pen to paper. His sympathy for the poor is one of his major virtues and his portraits of criminals and low-life in general are the most powerful things in his books. Mendelssohn's music may not throb with this kind of power, but, even so, we really must rethink the whole meaning of "Victorian" as it applies both to Dickens and to Mendelssohn.

Mendelssohn's family lineage was illustrious. His grandfather was the great Jewish philosopher Moses Mendelssohn, and his father, Abraham, was a noted banker. After Felix's star rose to such heights in the musical world, his father remarked ruefully, "When I was young, I was known as the son of my father; now I am known as the father of my son."

Some confusion stems from the fact that Felix

Mendelssohn's name is sometimes still listed on concert programs as Mendelssohn-Bartholdy. This stems from a relative of his father's who wanted the family to abandon its name as well as its religion and offered to bestow his own name on the whole lot. Felix, however, seems to have resisted the idea, preferring to be known by his original family name.

Probably the worst thing that ever happened to Felix Mendelssohn came 90 or so years after his death, when the Nazi regime in Germany sought to erase his name from musical history because of his Jewish origin. His statue in Leipzig was pulled down, his name disappeared from music-history texts, performances of his music were strictly forbidden and a suitably "Aryan" composer was commissioned to compose new incidental music to A Midsummer Night's Dream to replace his.

The German-born conductor Christoph von Dohnanyi once explained wryly how this situation gained him an accidental reputation as a Mendelssohn "specialist." Growing up in Germany during those terrible years, he and his fellow music students were forbidden any acquaintance with Mendelssohn's music, so when it became available again after the war he began investigating it with great gusto. He was asked to make a number of recordings of it, and before he knew it he had been tagged as a Mendelssohn "champion," a title to which he had never aspired.

On a visit to Berlin some years ago, I myself saw a reflection of German ambivalence to Mendelssohn that persists even to this day. As our tour bus passed the Dreifaeltigkeit (Holy Trinity) Cemetery, the tour guide remarked rather cryptically that he would tell us something that very few Berliners themselves know — Felix Mendelssohn lay buried in that cemetery. I made a mental note to return there on my own and find the grave.

Later when I asked the guide why he had said such a curious thing, he replied only that "Germans do not like history."

Eventually I found my way back to the place and located the grave — or rather the two graves — for Mendelssohn is interred there alongside his beloved sister Fanny. She was also a composer and her tombstone bears a line of her music chiseled in marble, and the words that go with it. Beside her, Felix's stone bears only his name and the dates 1809-1847. For all anyone could tell from that stone, he could have been a cab driver. Such a sad fate for a composer who wrote so much truly lovely music that continues to give pleasure to the world 150 years after his death!

Of course, what the Nazis did to Mendelssohn, to all other Jewish composers and to Jewish life and culture in general was a monstrous crime against not only art but against humanity. It shamed the great German artistic tradition. On the Allied side in both of the great world wars of this century there were moves against the music of Wagner, but these never went further than temporary banishment from the repertory, or, in some cases, performances of the Wagner operas in English only. Such things are certainly reprehensible, but in that regard they do not come anywhere near the Nazi actions, which were motivated by pure race hatred.

I have another and happier personal story to tell that involves Mendelssohn's music, however. It happened in 1947, the year of the centennial of the composer's death. Aged 17, I had spent a head-cracking Saturday taking college entrance examinations, and dragged myself home by subway and bus, wanting only to collapse from sheer exhaustion, unless by chance there might be supper before my collapse was complete.

During supper the phone rang. Someone had a spare ticket for that night's Boston Symphony concert, a special event marking the Mendelssohn anniversary: Midsummer Night's Dream excerpts, G major piano concerto, Italian symphony. I was out the door as though shot from a cannon, back onto bus and subway, and in Symphony Hall for the downbeat.

Wonderful evening. Have never forgotten it. Only after that did I remember to collapse properly.

When Mendelssohn was still quite young, his father determined that the whole family should convert from Judaism to Lutheranism, and they did so (this, of course, made no difference in later years to the Nazi guardians of Aryan racial purity). Felix thus wrote a great deal of Christian-oriented religious music that forms a significant part of his output. Of his two large-scale oratorios, Elijah deals with and Old Testament figure and Saint Paul, with one from the New Testament. I have no idea how personally devout Mendelssohn may have been, but his religious music forms an interesting case history in the long annals of the influence of religious literature and imagery on great composers. Bach, Bruckner, Dvorak and Messaien, for instance, were devout believers, and it shows in their music. Beethoven certainly believed in God, but his personal religion seems to have been a kind of pantheism or nature-worship that had nothing to do with regular churchgoing; yet he produced the marvelous Missa Solemnis using the church-Latin text and writing above the first measure mit andacht (with devotion). Brahms, an agnostic, wrote a deeply felt and beautiful Requiem according to his own idea of what a requiem should be. Frederick Delius, an aggressive and outspoken agnostic, went Brahms one degree better by writing a beautiful Requiem whose text explicitly denies the possibility of any life after death. Leos Janacek, who considered churches to be horrid places full of "bones and death" wrote a vivid and proclamatory Slavonic Mass that still thrills audiences today.

In our own day, consider the exotic religiously-oriented music of Olivier Messaien, a devout Catholic who was also influenced by Indian philosophy and birdsong, among many other things, and the sensuously beautiful religious music of Francis Poulenc, a man who almost seems in his music to have been two men, one a devout believer, the other a habitue of the cafes and music halls of Paris. Orthodox religious observance is obviously not a requirement for the creation of memorable religiously oriented music.

Mendelssohn's Elijah used to be a perennial favorite with oratorio societies and other assorted choral groups, professional and otherwise. It is not heard nearly so often nowadays as it used to be, which is a pity for it contains a good deal of truly lovely music, both in its large-scale choruses and in its solo arias. Saint Paul I find a harder nut to crack; it seems to me to be afflicted with a debilitating strain of pious stuffiness.

Some of Mendelssohn's very popular works — the delightful Italian Symphony, the violin concerto, the G minor piano concerto, the Midsummer Night's Dream music — stand today in danger of overexposure. They are trotted out at the slightest excuse by all sorts of performers and orchestras because they are sure-fire audience-pleasers and, being standard repertory, they are not likely to need extensive rehearsal. They are all splendid pieces that, so long as they are well performed, will tickle the ears of the patrons without unduly taxing their brain cells. The danger in the case of the two concertos is that all concerned will see them merely as virtuoso vehicles for showoff soloists, rather than as pieces that have other virtues to offer as well — which they do.

Music of a weightier sort — Beethoven symphonies are the best examples — can much better withstand the sort of constant repetition that has been the lot of these

Mendelssohn pieces. Mendelssohn's works, having less sheer depth and substance to them, tend to give way quicker in the listener's mind under the onslaught. Even so, everything Mendelssohn wrote for the orchestra is orchestrated with technical finesse, total transparency and lively imagination. He was no dilettante.

The Italian symphony is all sun, laughter and dancing; the Scottish has some picturesque seascape music in it. The Reformation symphony, despite a vein of earnest preachment that breaks through its surface here and there, is also a rousing and beautiful piece of music.

Mendelssohn wrote a lot of polished chamber music and instrumental pieces that are fairly often heard. The splendid Trio in D minor mentioned earlier is perhaps the item most often heard. There are eight whole books of Songs Without Words that pianists might explore with more imagination than they usually do (there is more there than the ubiquitous Spring Song).

Among Mendelssohn's lesser-known works, orchestras might consider more frequent performances of the liquidly delicious Fair Melusine overture. Like his far more popular Fingal's Cave overture it is water-music, though not on anything like so pictorial a scale; nonetheless, it is a charming piece. Also worth occasional hearings are some of the little string symphonies that Mendelssohn composed as a boy of about 12. They are very accomplished juvenilia, indeed — one of the few examples of that class of music that can be played and enjoyed on standard programs alongside more mature music, whether Mendelssohn's own or that of other composers.

For many years I was puzzled by the attribution of the famous Christmas carol Hark, the Herald Angels Sing to Mendelssohn; it did not seem to be listed anywhere in his output. Some sleuthing turned up a curious fact. The carol had been adapted from a male chorus that Mendelssohn wrote to help celebrate the 400th anniversary of, of all things, the invention of printing! Its original words were in praise of Gutenberg. I have never since that day been able to sing that carol with quite a straight face.

Aside from a single youthful effort that has not held the stage, Mendelssohn never really tried opera. His temperament seems in retrospect ill suited to the wild passions and unbridled emotional excesses of (most) opera, and he lived beyond the time when mere pretty tunes and beautiful singing could make stageable opera. Perhaps he realized this. His exact contemporary, Chopin, loved opera passionately (though he, too, never wrote one) and recommended that pianists seeking to learn how properly to interpret his piano music go and listen to the great Italian singers of the day. This advice would perhaps work only to a limited extent with Mendelssohn's music. You could fairly easily concoct a selection of Chopin's piano music that would contain a good deal more implicit "operatic" drama than almost anything of Mendelssohn's. It is curious that another undeniably great composer contemporary with

Mendelssohn and Chopin, Robert Schumann, also failed in his single attempt at an opera.

Mendelssohn's place in the modern repertory is secure. Even in times when it was looked down upon by the cognoscenti, it was still played quite frequently (it has this in common with Tchaikovsky). There will always be a place on concert programs for music of taste, fine workmanship, refinement and uncomplicated pleasure.

In recommending Mendelssohn for his refinement and elegance I do not mean to be damning him with faint praise. He is the perfect illustration of the fact that not all worthwhile works of music are necessarily works of high seriousness and boiling passion. He built elegant chauteaux and lovely houses, not great cathedrals. We need those cathedrals, to be sure, but we also need good houses. Better to aim at building fine houses and turn the trick consistently than to try to build cathedrals and not make the grade.

INTERLUDE II: Some Thoughts on Opera

Of all the (supposedly) mysterious corners of the world of classical music, none holds more terrors for the uninitiated than opera. Over its 400 years of existence, opera has developed a mystique all its own (which can certainly be a good thing), and also a reputation for elitist snobbery (which is the reverse side of the coin, and obviously a bad thing).

I approach this subject as an avowed opera lover of well over half a century's standing — but also as one with decidedly personal views on the subject, views that may not be very fashionable these days.

Seemingly everyone who writes or speaks on this complex art form shares one ultimate goal — to infect others with his own enthusiasm. Some, alas, go about the job in ways that seem to me to have the precise opposite effect, even though, as W. S. Gilbert puts it, "their intentions are well-meant." Like certain preachers, in trying to spread the good news they succeed only in alienating people from it.

The litany of charges leveled against opera by its legion of detractors is depressingly familiar: absurd plots sung in foreign languages by singers who cannot act; unrealistic dramatic situations made even more unrealistic by being stretched out on the Procrustean bed of music; a surfeit of gloomy tragic stories and an inordinately high death toll; the need to "do your homework" in advance in a way that is unnecessary when you go to the spoken theater or to the movies; the arcane shoptalk of hard-core devotees, most of it devoted to the relative merits of singers, and most of it conducted in a patois that to the average outsider might as well be Choctaw.

You can easily add your own pet peeve to the above list. There are plenty to choose from, though not all of them really matter.

Opera was invented by accident around 1600 by a group of Florentine noblemen who thought they were recreating the way Greek dramas were performed by their first interpreters. Almost from the beginning the operatic art form has been subject to criticism by the very people most concerned with it, the composers. Monteverdi, Gluck, Mozart and Wagner, just to name the most obvious names, each left opera a quite different thing than it had been when he received it. They were all "reformers," but the important thing is that each of them left us great operas that hold the stage today. They were not academic theorists, they were practitioners of the art of opera who decided it needed changing, and we still enjoy the results of their labors today.

Much of the controversy has swirled around the question of the relative importance in opera of words and music. In a sense, the creative tension between them is what opera is really all about.

Over the years, too, there has been a succession of ruling classes in the opera world — first the singers were the bosses, then the moneyed or titled patrons, then the conductors; today many claim that the stage directors are running the show. Unfortunately, there has never been any significant period of time in the 400-year history of opera when the composers — those who actually create the product — were kings of the mountain.

I regard this as an unfortunate truth, for my own view of opera is that it is basically a musical art form. Sure it involves poetry, acting, drama, dance, scene painting, stagecraft, costuming, makeup, lighting and various other constituent elements. But all those others must inevitably play subsidiary roles to the supremacy of music. An opera without a striking or memorable musical score is a frame without a painting. I believe that if we approach opera first and foremost as a musical experience, most of its terrors evaporate and we see clearly where its appeal lies and why it has lasted so long and prospered so well despite all its detractors. All those other elements have their place, but they cannot make the form work in the absence of great music.

Richard Wagner put the theory of opera as a union

of all the arts into words or, rather, into one jaw-breaking German word that may sound to the non-German like a burst of battlefield small-arms fire: Gesamtkunstwerk, the "total" or "all-inclusive" work of art. He wrote voluminously about this, but the fact remains that had he not filled his operas with sublimely beautiful and moving music, none of them would be alive today.

The standard piece of advice for someone encountering opera for the first time is to familiarize himself with the story before going, so he will know what is going on even though it is probably being sung in a foreign language. This is true so far as it goes, but equally important — indeed more important in my view — is the need for the opera-goer to familiarize himself with the music in advance, so that when he hears it in live performance it will come to him as an old and welcome friend happily encountered in perhaps unfamiliar circumstances. With each rehearing, whether in the opera house, on records or via radio or television, the music sinks deeper into one's consciousness, becomes more familiar and more meaningful. Eventually it becomes part of you — you own it inwardly and can call it up in memory at will.

Repeated hearings also teach you how the music reflects, comments upon, or illuminates the dramatic situation. You see how the composer was stimulated by the drama to clothe it in music that heightens and vivifies it.

This is the real answer to the argument that opera

is unrealistic and artificial. The exact reverse is true: opera heightens and intensifies reality. It has the power to make unreality real. It is the chief catalyst of the most vivid form of theater there is — the theater of the imagination. It takes human emotions and human dramatic situations as its starting point, and renders them incredibly more vivid than they are when considered for their own sake. The old cliche got it exactly right, music does indeed begin where words leave off.

A specific example might make this point clear. Let's take one from one of the most familiar and beloved of all operas, Verdi's Aida.

Toward the close of the third act of that masterpiece, poor Aida, the captive slave girl, has been persuaded by her father Amonasro, captive king of the defeated Ethiopians, to trick her lover, the Egyptian general Radames, into revealing his army's secret battle plans. Amonasro hides and overhears Aida's conversation with Radames. From Amonasro's point of view, all goes well; Radames asks Aida to flee with him and she craftily asks him what path they must take to avoid meeting the Egyptian army. Radames mentions the name of the gorges the army will be using to advance against the Ethiopians — the Gorges of Napata – whereupon Amonasro does something totally illogical. He strides from his hiding place, announces grandly that he is the Ethiopian king, that he has heard every word and that his troops will be there to meet the Egyptians!

Was there ever a stupider, a more incompetent spy?

Amonasro should, for obvious reasons, keep quiet and remain concealed. The whole episode is utterly ludicrous in any kind of realistic dramatic terms. Just for openers — how, pray, is Amonasro going to get the word to his far distant troops by the very next morning? A logical question in the dull factual sense, certainly; but in opera, an irrelevant one.

Just listen to the music Verdi has invented for this moment: the dramatic pronouncement of Amonasro, the stunned amazement and disbelief of poor Radames, the tension felt by Aida herself — all are brilliantly conveyed in a few bold musical strokes. There is simply no question of dramatic incongruity. This episode would be laughable in a stage play or   a movie, even in a novel. The only thing that makes it not only believable but also actually thrilling, is the power of Verdi's music. QED.

It is a relatively simple matter to familiarize yourself with the story of an opera before you go to hear it. The shelves of libraries are stuffed to bursting with books that can perform that service for you in as much detail as you require. There are quick and easy summaries, there are more detailed act-by-act, scene-by-scene guides. You can easily procure the libretti (full texts) themselves and read them over (beware, though, of bad translations. Most of the libretti available in libraries are still of ancient vintage and contain English translations that are risibly old-fashioned in addition to being frequently inaccurate. It is only in comparatively recent years that some really good translations of standard operas into modern English have begun to appear).

This brings us, inevitably, to the subject of translations projected on a screen in the opera house during the performance — the same technique used for foreign-language films. These are variously called surtitles, supertitles, or what-have-you, and they have very quickly established themselves as a standard feature in regional opera houses all over the world.

When this technique was first introduced in the 1970s it was very controversial. There was a sharp, but very short, controversy over its usefulness, which ended with the complete rout of the anti-supertitles faction. The tactic is now an accepted part of the operatic scene. Nonetheless, I remain opposed to it. I consider the projections a distraction from the music. I believe that opera-goers should do their homework before arriving for the performance so they can assimilate and enjoy the performance without having to do a lot of neck craning and head nodding.

This reactionary stance marks me as a hopeless Neanderthal savage somehow still left roaming the vast operatic prairie. There are just a few of us still around, and we are now mere powerless curiosities. As the comic poet Ogden Nash once said, "It's kind of fun to be extinct."

Once your need to know the outlines of an operatic story has been satisfied, it is time to get to work on the music. You can use CDs containing individual arias, "highlights" discs or complete recordings; if you are musically literate you can get scores from many libraries and noodle away at them yourself, literally teaching yourself the music in the most immediate and personal way. You can seek out knowledgeable friends and get from them some tips on what to listen for in a given work. What is important is that you bring to the performance a musical road map of some sort.

For pursuing this process of familiarization there is no substitute for simply listening to these operas on radio or on records. You can do it at one sitting or in smaller increments, act by act or even scene by scene. The power of the music will gradually do its work and you will be hooked.

The opera repertory is incredibly varied. It is a supermarket of styles, from the formal and somewhat formulaic construction of the earliest operas (culminating in the three extant masterpieces by Claudio Monteverdi), through the "reform" operas of Gluck to the supreme achievements of Mozart, Verdi, Wagner, Puccini, Strauss and others and on into the early modern era (Moussorgsky, Debussy, Berg, Poulenc) and the experimental works of today's composers. It is important for the beginning opera fan to follow his own inclinations, to pursue what appeals to him personally, and not feel constrained by peer pressure to investigate every single school unless he wants to.

Opera seems somehow more prone to impassioned peer-pressure advocacy than other departments of the classical music world. Opera fans can be the worst kind of zealots, each pushing his own favorite work or, more likely, favorite singer at the expense of everyone else's. Often they tend not to be at all interested in other kinds of classical music; many of them don't go to symphony concerts, chamber music or solo instrumental recitals. It is important for the neophyte to make up his own mind and not to be swayed by propaganda, even propaganda from respected and knowledgeable sources.

Personal tastes being as varied as they are, it would be futile to simply lay down a list of favorite operas that a newcomer to the form might want to seek out. Those that are my personal favorites might put someone else to sleep. It is possible, though, to lay down a few general principles to guide the inquisitive but, perhaps, inexperienced listener.

You can always start with the appealingly human and musically seductive operas of Puccini, works of enduring popularity and immense musical effectiveness. I think, in general, they are likely to seduce the ears of most listeners who come to them without much experience. Five or six of them are so immensely popular that they are easily available, whether in live performance, recordings or radio broadcasts.

The great (and also immensely popular) middle-period operas of Verdi – Rigoletto, Il Trovatore and La Traviata for sure, four or five others following in their wake - might also come early in the regimen.

If your interest lies mainly in the voice and vocal

melody, the products of the Italian bel canto tradition might be worth early investigation — the famous and popular operas of Rossini, Bellini and Donizetti. Donizetti's famous Lucia di Lammermoor is a quintessential example. Musically the greatest of these works, I feel, is Bellini's Norma, but it is not as easily encountered and is not as varied in mood and style as is the more approachable Lucia.

Mozart's great operas (six or seven of them are in today's standard repertory) are unsurpassed for sheer musical genius poured out in a veritable flood; but they lie a notch or two higher in the degree of musical sophistication and careful listening that they require. Disarmingly charming and "simple" as they appear on their surfaces, these works have hidden depths that the beginning ear may miss.

To repeat a point made earlier, Mozart was the greatest natural-born musical genius who ever lived. His operas are incredibly sophisticated masterworks, but they take a practiced ear to get the most out of them. They are works that can be enjoyed on many levels, not all of them immediately obvious to the casual ear.

As the listener gains in experience and confidence, he can begin to approach the great mountain range of Richard Wagner's operas, the later Verdi, the more "modernistic" products of Richard Strauss. By the time you reach that level you are ready to strike out on your own, to explore other byways of the repertory (Russian, American, Czech, British, the lesser-known French operas that lie beyond Carmen and Faust, the fascinating field of post-1950 opera). These are merely a few general suggestions to get you started.

One of the sillier prejudices still abroad in the music world has it that operatic music, by and large, is somehow "inferior" to the symphonic variety. Composers like Verdi and Puccini (though not Wagner!), who worked fairly exclusively in opera, are often denigrated as somehow unworthy of comparison with the great symphonic giants. This is patent nonsense and should not deter anyone from the enjoyment of opera. There is too much great music composed for the opera medium to allow any such silly attitude to get in its way.

I feel too that entirely too much energy is wasted among opera fans in fruitless arguments and comparisons over singers. This seems to be the favorite indoor sport of opera lovers, but it is one in which subjectivity reigns supreme. Two opera-goers can sit side by side and hear the same cast in the same opera — and come away with diametrically opposed views as to who made the grade and who did not. Given the long history of the genre, too, much evidence from the past has to be based on old and imperfect phonograph records which may or may not give an accurate impression of what voices sounded like and how personalities were projected in the live-performance experience.

No one can deny that fine singing is a thrilling experience and that good singing (at the very least) is a sine qua non for a good performance. But I do believe that the constant focusing on singers (and on personalities in general) has tended to turn the opera house into a bullfight arena and the opera audience into the crowd at a sports event rather than the audience for a genuinely moving artistic experience. What is needed for deep and lasting enjoyment of the form, I feel (and again I am distinctly in the minority) is more concentration on the work itself rather than on the performers. The work itself, specifically its music, is what really matters. No one would condone poor performances, of course; but it seems silly to prize spectacular singing when it purveys inferior music. Opera listeners should be more than mere "canary fanciers."

Opera is one of the great modern inventions, and it has brought more joy and inspiration into more lives over the past 400 years than many another one could name. It is one of the world's great beneficial addictions.

VII. RICHARD WAGNER (1813-1883)

We really must deal here with two related but separate entities — the Wagner that concertgoers meet in the concert hall, and the Wagner who inhabits the opera house itself. The former, alas, has the bigger public, but it is really not possible to understand the man, his musical modus operandi or his true greatness until you have encountered him in his natural theatrical setting.

Perhaps there is even a third Wagner lurking about here, a shadowy, insubstantial figure created by the political events of the past 60 years and the utterly unpredictable two-way interaction that fatefully linked those events with a composer who had been in his grave for half a century when they began to unfold.

Much learned musicological ink used to be spilled discussing "the Wagner question," i.e., Richard Wagner's final place in musical history. That debate is long since over; even those who loathe both the man and his music have long since conceded that he was more than a great composer, he was one of those seminal figures who changed music forever. Wagner was a kind of one-man musical earthquake that rearranged the aesthetic landscape overnight. If you must set down a specific date for the beginning of that dreaded apparition, "modern music," try June 10, 1865, when Tristan und Isolde was first heard. Its famous prelude has been described as the first extended piece of music whose key is indefinite, and the equally famous "Tristan chord" that comes in its second measure still perplexes academic analysts.

"Wagner nights" are not as common in our concert halls as they used to be, and very few Wagner arias are ever heard in recital any more, even when the recitalist is a certified opera star. There are, however, plenty of available discs of Wagner excerpts, and a large segment of the public that would regard attendance at a Wagner opera performance as the equivalent of root canal work listens to those excerpts with great pleasure. There are millions out there who know the Prelude and the Liebestod from Tristan but have not the foggiest notion of the three and a half hours of music that lies between them. Even reputable conductors have presided over pre-cooked orchestral versions of Ring excerpts on a single compact disc as though this constituted an acceptable substitute for knowing the whole cycle.

I cheerfully admit to a purist bias here. I prefer Wagner served up musically whole rather than in tiny morsels — George Szell used to call them "bleeding chunks" — torn from their operatic contexts. Some of these morsels are delicious indeed, but they gain ever so much more both musically and dramatically when heard in their proper contexts. Who are these smug deities crossing that rainbow bridge into Valhalla at the end of Das Rheingold and why are they headed for big trouble despite the brave sounds Wagner's orchestra makes? What exactly is Isolde singing about in that ravishing Liebestod just before she dies? What is the significance of that peaceful Good Friday morn music in the third act of Parsifal?

Nonetheless, even in these out-of-context concert excerpts, some important things about Wagner as a revolutionary composer are on view, for example:

* We can hear how he silvered and ennobled for all time the sound of the opera orchestra, even inventing special instruments to achieve the effects he wanted. No such eloquent orchestration had ever before been heard in the history of music.

* We can hear how he stretched the bounds of harmony, bringing it to a level of chromatic complexity previously unknown in music.

* We can hear, if only to a limited extent in concert excerpts, the play and interplay of the system of leitmotivs out of which he wove his orchestral fabric. These are short, highly descriptive musical phrases meant to stand for characters, objects, emotions, places and even abstract philosophical ideas that figure in the Wagnerian plots.

* We can (if there are vocal soloists) gain some idea

of the new balance between voice and orchestra that he established. This crucial factor in the history of opera fluctuates even within his works, of course, depending on the dramatic situation; but in general the Wagnerian singer's voice floats on a rich moving stream of orchestral sound like a small boat carried along by a swift river. Sometimes it is a placid river, sometimes a roaring torrent, but the sense of movement, of being carried along is always there.

All of these factors, of course, have their effect magnified many times in full-length performance.

Wagner constructed his vast music dramas according to his own self-evolved system, and, being Wagner, he elaborated that system in a number of long-winded prose essays. The basic principal was that in his operas the text (always written by himself) and its meaning were of paramount importance; the music — and every other aspect of the performance — were all there mainly to help make clear the meaning of that text. The whole thing was to constitute a single entity, which Wagner christened with a resounding German title: Gesamtkunstwerk, the "total work of art," a union of all the arts in one interrelated whole.

That sounds just fine, but the fact is that Wagner's lasting greatness rests on the fact that he contradicted his own theory. His operas are not celebrated today because of their texts, and they are not in any meaningful way unions of all the arts. They are surpassingly great works of music. Wagner was a supreme composer but a mediocre poet, and his sense of theater is open to serious question. It is because he clothed his texts in immortal music that they are alive today. The Ring, Tristan, Meistersinger, or Parsifal with music by some lesser composer would be inconceivable.

Nowadays, I admit, this is an unfashionable view. We live in the age of opera-as-theater, when the visual side of opera production has attained an importance previously undreamed of. There are even those who think it has usurped the primacy of music in the operatic mix.

I maintain stubbornly that this is nonsense. Operas today, like their predecessors in every period of operatic history, live and die by their music. If its music is worthy, or at least if it affords juicy opportunities for singers to show off what they can do, an opera has a shot at survival. I know of no opera that survives in the standard repertory solely because it has a superior libretto. The criteria for admission to this Valhalla are strictly musical and Richard Wagner possessed them to an extraordinary degree. That is why his operas flourish. A fine staged production of a Wagner opera can enhance the musical effect, but a poor one cannot destroy that effect, if the music is well performed.

One of the major advantages — indeed, perhaps the major advantage of the full-length Wagner production over the concert excerpts is simply that there is so much glorious music in these operas that you will literally never hear unless you go for the live performance or the complete recording. Examples flock to mind:

* The duet between Ortrud and Telramund at the start of act 2 of Lohengrin, culminating in the terrifying unison of Der Rache Werk, (The task of vengeance) one of the most vivid expressions of pure malevolence in all music.

* The superb scene between Wotan and Fricka early in act two of Die Walkure.

*The lovely scene between Sachs and Eva in the second act of Meistersinger.

*The great orchestral passage between the two scenes of the last act of Siegfried that propels Siegfried through the magic fire and leads him to Brunnhilde on the mountaintop.

That list could go on at numbing length, if I would let it. If I had command of a symphony orchestra somewhere (and barrels of money to boot), I would devise for it a whole series of such extended Wagnerian excerpts other than the ones we commonly hear. They are there, immured in Wagner's scores, waiting to find the larger public they deserve. They are musical buried treasures.

Even more persuasive, perhaps would be a second list of much briefer moments, tiny Wagnerian bits that illuminate a phrase, an action, and even sometimes a single word. Each listener will have his own stockpile of such small gems; they are strewn through the scores like stars in the night sky and you will never hear them in programs limited to the standard Wagnerian snippets. I could name several dozen such epiphanies from my own personal list without thinking twice, and new ones keep appearing with each re-hearing of a familiar score.

I am convinced that many of those who still profess to dislike Wagner are people who have seldom if ever listened to him at any length. They are condemning something they do not really know — a situation all too prevalent these days in fields far removed from art, alas, as in art itself.

Which leads us to the inevitable question of Richard Wagner and the misuse of his music by evil men in his own country long after his death. The old "Wagner Question," dealing with the intrinsic worth of his music, has long since been laid to rest; but it has been succeeded by a new and far thornier "Wagner Question," asked in all seriousness by people who see in his personal life and in his operas the seeds of Nazi racial theories, specifically of virulent anti-Semitism. This "Wagner Question" is still a long way from final settlement. It has soured many intelligent and otherwise musically tolerant people on Wagner's music. It is not in any real sense a "musical" question, but it is a serious matter that must be dealt with.

Everyone will have a unique personal response to this matter. I can only give you mine.

First, the reactions of those who suffered from the Nazi tyranny, either themselves or through their families, must be understood and respected. There can be no whitewashing of the enormous crime that was committed. What is legitimately at issue is the extent to which Wagner, who died six years before Adolf Hitler was born, may be logically implicated in this crime.

Wagner was, of course, a virulent anti-Semite and a fervent German nationalist. These were both ideas espoused by the Nazi regime also, and the Nazis found in Wagner's prose writings and operas a kind of convenient scriptural foreshadowing of both ideas — the work of a great master from the German past which they could twist to their own ideological uses.

It was, of course, a perversion of Wagner's work. The Nazis noted Wagner's operatic quest for a great "hero" who would restore the glory of the old German gods, and equated that with their loathsome ideas about Aryan racial "purity." What they forgot to do was to check the end of Götterdammerung and to note what became of their "hero" in the end, and of the whole world, both human and godly, that he inhabited. The "hero" was murdered, literally stabbed in the back, and the gods were destroyed. The "new order" thus established was to be based on justice — on the restoration of stolen property (the ring) to its rightful owners (the Rhinemaidens), and not on crackpot racial theories. The Nazis might well have pondered this, but they did not.

Wagner, as stated above, was a fervent German nationalist, but his nationalism was based on a reverence for the German past. He believed firmly in the energizing power of myth as a means of showing a searching people where it came from and what its destiny might be, hence the four mighty Ring operas, the greatest work of art in the entire history of man that is entirely the work of a single person.

His reverence for the German past also had a shorter-range focus. This is evident in Die Meistersinger, which affectionately evokes, in both music and text, Germany as it was 300 years before Wagner lived. For the Germans and the Germany of his own day, Wagner had little use, as one can see from his own writings and from the published diaries of his wife Cosima.

The Nazis, being basically stupid, missed all this and distorted Wagner into a simple-minded prop for their own follies. I do not feel that Wagner can be held responsible for this. His personal anti-Semitism was a gross blot on his character, but it can hardly be tagged as the reason for the existence of Auschwitz.

I concur heartily with Daniel Barenboim's remark that some of those who still equate Wagner with Nazi ideas seem to believe that Richard Wagner was living in Berlin in 1940. Someone else remarked trenchantly that blaming Wagner for the Nazi excesses would be rather like blaming Christ for the Spanish Inquisition.

Much of the anti-Wagner feeling that persists on these political grounds has its origin in highly personal memories of terrible deeds committed long ago. No one that did not experience these horrors has the right to condemn outright those who did; but I think that Wagner's transcendent music has survived the mud spattered on it by the Nazis just as it survived the sneers of critics in its own day.

Listening to concert excerpts from Wagner's operas can be relatively easy. The gorgeous orchestration, melodic richness and sheer eloquence of the music unfailingly do their work and the listener is seduced. Listening to the full-length operas, however, can be difficult. They are undeniably long, and productions of them outside our relatively few major operatic centers are still rather infrequent — though thankfully not so rare as they used to be. You are more likely than before to encounter Tannhauser in Sarasota or Walküre in Phoenix, and such opportunities should be grasped whenever possible, provided the productions seem likely to do the works justice.

The other route, of course, is the complete recording. The whole Wagner canon is available by now on compact discs that can be bought or borrowed from a library. In a way, this may even be a better way for the listener just beginning to explore Wagner to make the acquaintance of these wonderful works. You can listen to as much or as little at a sitting as you wish, and you can have libretto (or perhaps even score) before you as you listen. The close interrelation of music and text in Wagner's work will become crystal clear, and you can make note on the spot of specific passages that especially take your fancy. Also, such listening calls into play the imagination, a faculty once much prized but fallen into disrepute in this television age. You do not have to settle for some stage director's inadequate version of the ride of the Valkyries or the Tristan love duet; you can see it realized perfectly in the most wonderful theater there is, the one that exists in your own mind.

The only warning I would issue is that these works, once approached, explored and (more or less) comprehended whole, are highly addictive. Wagner's glorious music is a kind of drug that may temporarily dull your taste for the operas of other composers. Like most intoxications, this one will wear off and you will regain your love for Mozart, Verdi or Bellini; but the process can take time, and it can turn you temporarily into a truly obnoxious musical snob. Wagner's scores and record albums should come equipped with medical-style warnings about possible side effects.

After the side effects wear off, however, the long-term benefits will make themselves felt. You will spend the rest of your life plumbing the depths of these musical oceans, like some artistic scuba diver given the opportunity to map the floor of the entire Pacific. It is a lifetime, not of work, but of incredible joy and inspiration.

VIII. GUSTAV MAHLER (1860-1911)

It is indeed fitting that one of Mahler's massive symphonies, his second, bears the title Resurrection , for no composer's reputation has undergone so startling a resurrection in recent years as his. He whose music was once dismissed as long-winded, self-centered and neurasthenic now stands proudly at the very center of the symphonic repertory all over the world. In his own lifetime, contemplating his less than stellar reputation as a composer, Mahler said simply "mein zeit wird gekommen" (my time will come). It certainly has.

Obviously, this remarkable reversal of critical and public opinion is primarily due to the eloquence and power of the music itself. Mahler also was fortunate, however, in gaining some very influential conductors as champions, first people like Willem Mengelberg and Bruno Walter, and later the charismatic Leonard Bernstein. Another decisive factor in Mahler's rehabilitation surely was the invention of the long-playing (LP) record about 1947. This event meant that finally all of Mahler's outsize symphonies became available to record buyers in a practical format. At precisely that historical moment, his reputation took off.

Until that happened, the public's chances to become acquainted with most of Mahler's work were very sketchy indeed. Of the symphonies, only the first and fourth, plus the song-symphony Das Lied von der Erde were known to anything like a wide public. The first and fourth symphonies are the only two among Mahler's nine that clock in at less than an hour of performance time. They call for relatively modest orchestral forces in Mahlerian terms, and the fourth is certainly the most immediately genial and approachable of all the nine. The first symphony, certainly the most startlingly original first symphony in all of music, was heard a good deal, but it was still regarded as something of a curiosity. Das Lied von der Erde was in the repertory and had a public, but its attraction was often based on the identity of the two singers who shared its six songs.

The fifth symphony was heard now and then, and some of Mahler's songs were occasionally heard, either with orchestra or in recital with piano. The Songs of a Wayfarer and Songs on the Death of Children came along at rare intervals. But in toto, the situation hardly represented a fair sampling of the man's output.

Critics in general were dismissive. Mahler was a hypersensitive egomaniac and a self-indulgent bore, the kind of fellow who grabs you by the lapel at a party, fixes you with a wild stare and starts pouring out his troubles, while you look around in vain for an escape route. The symphonies were thin in musical substance, bombastic and repetitive, hardly worth the investment of time it took to listen to them.

In those days of the 78-rpm record, with its four minutes and twenty seconds per side, there was little recorded evidence to prove or disprove this verdict. I own to this day a 78-rpm recording of the second symphony made in 1936 by Eugene Ormandy and what was then the Minneapolis Symphony. It takes up 22 record sides, and those 11 discs are indeed a bulky and heavy armful. In those days, if you wanted one of the lengthy Mahler symphonies on 78-rpm (assuming that it had been recorded in the first place) it would have been a good idea to take a wheelbarrow to the record store.

With the invention of the LP record this situation was corrected overnight. The big — and largely unknown — Mahler symphonies emerged from their solitary confinement cells to be judged on their own merits and not on the say-so of often hostile critics and musicologists. The second, fifth and ninth came first, soon followed by the lengthy third, and finally by the least known of the lot, the tragic sixth and the enigmatic seventh. Even the gigantic eighth symphony, with its vast army of choristers and soloists, was performed, broadcast and recorded in due time.

Mahler was fortunate, too, in the timing of this emergence. His music knocked at the door of the standard repertory at a time when self-questioning and seeking after answers to cosmic riddles were very much in the air. The Second World War was over, but the Cold War had begun and there was much uncertainty about personal and political goals, not to mention personal and political futures. The specter of the atomic bomb hung over the world. No one knew where we were headed. Mahler's angst-ridden music spoke to that mood. Even the final sense of triumphant certitude that one hears at the close of the second and third symphonies came to the listener only after a long and arduous journey through doubt and even despair.

Mahler's name was often, and still is, linked with that of his fellow Austrian Anton Bruckner (1824-1896), who also had written nine large-scale symphonies. But, as a glance at their dates will show, the two men were not really contemporaries, and their personalities, outlook on life and musical style could hardly have been more different.

Mahler was continually tortured by doubt and guilt feelings; Bruckner was a serene and rather simple fellow, a devout believer in a benevolent Catholic God. Mahler's life was a series of melodramatic crises; Bruckner's was uneventful (he spent most of it as a church organist). Mahler's love life was the stuff of lurid soap opera; Bruckner never married (though he did have an embarrassing habit of proposing marriage to much younger girls, some of whom he only knew casually — supermarket tabloid fodder rather than soap opera!)

What seems significant about this Odd Couple is that Mahler's wildly confessional music gained a large public in the unsettled postwar years; Bruckner was sort of towed along in Mahler's wake, but never achieved any comparable level of spontaneous public acceptance. Even today, though his stock may be much higher than it was in the pre-LP age, it still stands nowhere near the level of Mahler's. For better or worse. Mahler's feverish questioning and doubting seem to mean more to more of us than does Bruckner's serene, shining faith.

Mahler and Richard Strauss stand at an important musical crossroads. They helped to move music from the post-Wagnerian late-Romantic era toward the modern age. In this Strauss, who lived until 1949, was far in advance of Mahler — but there are patches in Mahler's music too that certainly point the way toward the future. Neither man, it seems obvious, could have spoken with the voice he did had not Richard Wagner existed first.

Few if any composers reflect their innermost personal passions in their music as directly as Mahler does. He even occasionally left passionate exclamations scrawled on his manuscripts that gave clues as to what sort of inner emotional event was driving his inspiration at that point. It is certainly not necessary to know what these emotional triggers were in order for us to be moved by the music today. It is enough to know that the composition of these extraordinary pieces was a kind of catharsis for this sensitive and deeply wounded human being.

Some sense of the alienation in which much of Mahler's music is grounded comes when we consider his famous statement about himself: I am, he said, three times an exile: as a Bohemian in Austria, as an Austrian among Germans and as a Jew in the world. No one, for instance, can listen to the final movement of the sixth symphony, a work that ends in utter catastrophe after many fleeting glimpses of hope, without feeling that this is a man at the end of his rope.

Mahler believed, too, that a symphony, as a kind of personal confessional diary, had to be inclusive rather than exclusive. His effort was to put absolutely everything into his music, rather than to pare it down to essentials. This accounts in some degree for the sheer length of the symphonies, and also for their often heterogeneous content. In them we hear, cheek by jowl, folk dances and folk-like tunes, military marches in abundance, imitations of nature (e.g., birdcalls), military bugle calls, Jewish klezmer strains, noble chorales, religious ecstasy — and of course symphonic strains by a composer who knew how to integrate his own style with all these other elements. The canvases are mostly large, the orchestral and choral forces required likewise. The extraordinary third symphony at an hour and 45 minutes is by a considerable margin the longest work entitled "symphony" that comes anywhere near being a standard repertory item today.

Mahler was a brilliantly imaginative orchestrator. He announced that fact in the very first measure of his first symphony, where we hear the note A sounded as softly as possible in unison through seven octaves. Over that extraordinary beginning Mahler wrote wie ein naturlaut (like a sound of nature), and so it is. It is as though the symphony does not so much begin as somehow materialize out of thin air. Mysterious horn calls and trumpet fanfares echo across the orchestra for several minutes. Something quite out of the ordinary is afoot, but the first-time listener has no clue as to exactly what. Then finally when Mahler drops this apocalyptic pose and begins his symphony proper, what do we hear – a folk-ditty! It is an orchestral version of one of his own naive songs of nature ("As I went through the fields in the morning..."). No composer in the long history of music had ever begun a first symphony this way. In the days before Mahler's time came, critics dismissed this sort of thing as an inappropriate mixing together of incompatible elements. Today we hear it differently and are swept away by its boldness. And in the same unconventional first symphony there was that weird third movement, beginning with a hollow rhythmic impulse in the timpani, over which is heard a mournful, minor-key variation on the famous Frere Jacques folk tune played by a solo double bass, an instrument seldom used for solos but projecting a tonal color like a low-pitched wail. The mock funeral dirge gives way to other episodes, including an unmistakable reference to the music of a Jewish village klezmer ensemble. The move-ment ends with a return of the Frere Jacques parody and the timpani rhythm, followed by a strident clash of cymbals, a hysterical outburst from the full orchestra, and a twenty-minute final movement of the most impassioned sort. This is clearly music that follows no rules but its own. Upon hearing a performance of this symphony as a young man, Bruno Walter decided on the spot that he simply had to meet the man who could compose such extravagant music; that meeting led to their close friendship and Walter's lifelong podium championship of Mahler's cause.

The symphonies that have benefited most from the reassessment of Mahler in recent years have probably been the ones that require massed voices, especially the magnificent second (Resurrection) symphony. The sheer length of the third symphony and the size of the performing forces required to do justice to the eighth have made them into special occasion pieces rather than integral parts of the standard repertory; but the second symphony, more modest in both length and size but equally extravagant in its emotional impact, has taken on the status of a popular favorite — and justly so, for it is a magnificent work.

Religious matters were always a major factor in Mahler's angst-ridden outlook. He was driven from the directorship of the Vienna State Opera in part because he was Jewish, and this question pursued him relentlessly all his life (he eventually converted to Christianity but his heart was not in it; inwardly he remained a Jew to the end.) The second symphony is a non-doctrinal and nondenominational statement of faith in life after death. We experience in its first three movements, first the terror of the fact of death, then reflections, first happy, then nervous and unsettling, on the life that has just ended. In the fourth movement the solo contralto poses the central question: What next? The extended finale is Mahler's answer, a ringing affirmation by orchestra, soloists and chorus of his belief that earthly death is not the end of everything.

The statement is purely personal. It has nothing whatever to do with any sectarian creed. It is quite simply one of the most consistently successful large-scale musical conceptions ever achieved by any composer, a 35-minute sweep that begins in terrifying, apocalyptic drama and ends with confident affirmation.

The least popular of the Mahler symphonies remain the sixth and seventh, two darkly colored purely orchestral works that show Mahler at his most emotionally tortured. Like all of Mahler's symphonies, they contain moments of joy and exaltation alongside moments of bitter despair. The sixth reflects a series of personal tragedies that struck Mahler as he was preparing to write it, including the discovery of his own ultimately fatal heart condition. The seventh contains two strikingly original "night-music" movements and a finale that is perhaps the most problematic single movement in any of the symphonies. It makes a brave noise, but there is something hollow and unconvincing about it, especially in a less-than-expert performance. Mahler bade his personal farewell to the world in the last movement of the ninth symphony, which fades away into an exhausted silence, and in Das Lied von der Erde, a work also tinged with fatalistic melancholia. He never lived to complete his tenth symphony, and performances today either rest content with the two movements he did complete or employ versions of the whole work put together from fragmentary sketches by other hands.

It would be a mistake, however, to judge Mahler only by these outsize major works. He is equally revealing of himself, and equally musically revolutionary, in his songs (several of the early symphonies make thematic use of some of these songs also).

Many of Mahler's songs exist in both orchestral and piano-accompaniment versions. There is no doubt that the extant superb orchestrations (some by Mahler himself, some by other hands) can lend them a special luster, but they are certainly not to be passed over when some recitalist who is on Mahler's expressive wavelength offers them in recital. A fine piano accompanist can constitute an orchestra with his ten fingers, and a great singer can make these superb songs live no matter what sort of accompaniment is available.

It is difficult to assemble a short list of the worthiest of Mahler's songs; it takes great self-restraint, since the quality level is so consistently high. My personal list would certainly include the lovely Ich atmet einen lindenduft (I breathe the linden tree's fragrance), the world-weary Ich bin der Welt Abhanden Gekommen (I am lost to the world), the sardonic Des Antonius vom Padua Fischpredigt (Saint Anthony preaching to the fish, a song also used as the basis for a movement in the second symphony), the humorous Wer hat dies Liedlein Erdacht? (Who composed this little song?), the lovely Liebst du um Schoenheit (If you love beauty), and certainly the transcendent Um Mitternacht (At Midnight), a song which travels the same road from doubt and fear to religious certitude as does the second symphony, but makes the trip in five minutes rather than 80.

The song-cycle Das Lied von der Erde is justly famous, but worth knowing also is an earlier cycle, Das Klagende Lied (Song of Complaint), especially as now outfitted with a newly discovered final section that was restored to it only in recent years.

Gustav Mahler, one of the greatest opera conductors who ever lived, and a man with more drama in his soul than most other people, never himself wrote an opera. His nearest approach was the preparation of a performing version of an obscure operetta by Carl Maria von Weber, Der Drei Pintos. Actually his nine huge symphonies form a kind of gigantic opera, with himself as the central character. He is a composer who speaks specifically to our own day and age as do few others in the canon. The critics were wrong. Mahler's time is here and now.

IX. RICHARD STRAUSS (1864-1949)

It is a familiar story in musical history: the composer who is regarded in his own lifetime as a wild-eyed radical but lives long enough to see himself enshrined as a "new-old" master. This has happened to Strauss (and Stravinsky) recently enough to be part of the collective memory of today's concertgoing audience. I well remember my own mother tut-tutting over some of Strauss' more extravagant orchestral moments (but, to be fair, in general she loved his music).

I have deep reservations about a number of Strauss' major works — reservations which will become apparent in this essay; yet there is no disputing his status as a major composer or his continuing hold on the concert-going public (two things that are not necessarily synonymous).

Strauss provides a convenient bridge to lead listeners from the twilight glow of late Romanticism into the perhaps artificial but no less intriguing light of the modern era. At the very end of his life, like many another old man, Strauss fell into a mood of nostalgic musing and penned two masterly works, the Metamorphosen for strings and the Four Last Songs, that hark back at least 50 years stylistically. In the Four Last Songs he even quotes from one of his own early works.

Strauss shares with Benjamin Britten the distinction of being a 20th-century master who made equal impact in both symphony hall and opera house. Both men wrote masterly songs, but Strauss clearly has the edge there; neither one was a major figure in chamber music, though Britten bulks a trifle larger.

Strauss was born into the flood-tide era of Richard Wagner's influence (he was 19 when Wagner died). His father, a virtuoso horn player, hated Wagner's music but was deeply involved with it — he had played horn in the orchestra at the world premiere of Tristan und Isolde. Thus it is no surprise that Strauss' early works bear the Wagnerian stamp. Every beginning artist, whether composer, writer, painter, what-have-you, begins by imitating models, and in Strauss' youth Wagner bestrode the whole musical world, a model that no one could escape.

The earliest Strauss work heard with any frequency today is the first of his two horn concertos, a piece written when he was a teenager (the second one came along some 60 years later!) Generally speaking, Strauss composed almost all of his great series of tone-poems that symphony-goers know today before turning with any great success to the field of opera; the only two of his tone-poems written after he began to write operas are the Symphonia Domestica and the Alpine Symphony, neither one generally ranked among his completely successful works (though the Domestica has some high-profile champions). The first of Strauss' major tone-poems, Don Juan, dates from 1888; Salome, the first of his operas to become a repertory item, was premiered in 1905.

The "tone-poem" had been invented by Franz Liszt around 1850. It is an orchestral piece based in some way on literature, an attempt to tell a story or illustrate a series of literary moods and situations in terms of pure music, without words. Strauss brought the form to an extraordinary state of complexity and musical sophistication, beginning somewhat tentatively with Aus Italien (From Italy), a kind of hybrid of symphony and symphonic poem. His reputation in the tone-poem form today is based on six major works that are part of the repertory of every major orchestra: Don Juan, Death and Transfiguration, Thus Spake Zarathustra, Till Eulenspiegel's Merry Pranks, Don Quixote and A Hero's Life.

They make up an extraordinary body of descriptive, often actually pictorial music. The bleating sheep and whirling windmill of Don Quixote are famously success-ful feats of turning the symphony orchestra into a kind of audible camera, so realistic is their reproduction in sound of the pictorial imagery. To these may be added the deathbed music that opens Death and Transfiguration,

the trial and graphic execution of poor Till, and most
certainly the grandiose sunrise episode that opens
Zarathustra (later adopted for use in a famous outer space
movie, 2001, and thus accorded something of a vogue on
the pop charts; many a 1960s movie-goer was astonished
to find that this famous passage was followed in Strauss'
original by some 35 more minutes of music).

What Strauss demonstrated in these astonishing
scores (which cover roughly a single decade, 1888-1898,
in his composing career) was an incredible command
of what a symphony orchestra could be made to do. To
begin with, he enlarged the orchestra itself, calling for a
number of unusual instruments and generally asking for
more of everything. The wind-machine in Don Quixote
and the rattle in Till Eulenspiegel got lots of publicity
at the time, but what was truly noteworthy was Strauss'
virtuoso writing for the standard instruments, notably
horns and winds in general. His scores show an incredible
amount of activity all over the orchestra in their moments
of high excitement. There are details in those scores
that cannot possibly come through to the listener as
individual sounds in performance, but what is important
is the overall effect, the general sense of bustle and
overflowing energy.

In these pieces, too, Strauss began the process of
expanding the bounds of post-Wagnerian harmony. He
did not hesitate to employ chords and progressions that
were then considered dissonant, and to carry Wagnerian
chromaticism a good deal further than Wagner himself

had. He completed this process in the operas that came later. This marks the beginning of the breakup of what most people even today consider "conventional" harmony.

Within individual pieces in this series of works there is a huge variation in style and quality. Moments of grace and refinement alternate with moments of vulgarity and coarseness. Strauss' creative faculty was incredibly fertile, but not very self-critical. Audiences today sit through some of the uninspired stretches (the battle music in Heldenleben, certain commonplace stretches in Till) for the sake of the inspiration and beauty with which they are surrounded. The most consistently successful of these pieces, to my mind, are Don Juan (shortest of the lot at about 16 minutes) and Zarathustra, despite the stern adverse judgments rendered against it by a good many critics over the years. All six pieces have wondrous things in them, but not all of them are uniformly successful.

Interesting, too, is the fact that Strauss cast several of these extended quasi-literary works in his own inflated versions of standard symphonic forms. Till Eulenspiegel is an outsize rondo, the form used for finale movements by Mozart, Haydn and other classical era composers. Don Quixote is a gargantuan theme and variations, and Heldenleben stretches the formal scheme of the first movement of a classical symphony (formally known as sonata-allegro form) over fifty minutes.

These pieces are now standard repertory. They have

lost the shock value that once inspired satirical verses and huffish letters to the editor. This is not quite so true of the Strauss operas, however; you could argue that at least two of them, Salome and Elektra, still possess some of the shock value, at least in regards to their music, that they had when they were new almost 90 years or more ago. Like all the arts, music does not move from style to style and from period to period in a straight line. There are wild leaps into the future and obvious looks back to the past. Salome and Elektra still sound very "modern" indeed to many listeners.

Of Strauss' fifteen operas, three are now standard repertory and another three or four turn up often enough to keep a toehold on the public consciousness.

Strauss' first two operas have not made it into the worldwide repertory, but in 1905 suddenly along came Salome, an almost verbatim setting of the decadent Oscar Wilde play (itself an elaboration of a Biblical incident) as rendered into flowery German. It made Strauss famous — and notorious — overnight. He was denounced as a sensation-monger because of his choice of subject matter, and as a musical anarchist because of the wildly colorful and passionate score he produced for it. Then just three years later he topped that with Elektra, an even more adventurous score on an even more lurid subject.

These are two extraordinarily powerful works, even today, when the controversy over their subject matter has long since ended. Under a conductor who can pace them properly, whipping them up to fever pitch at their dramatic climaxes, and with singers who can meet their heavy vocal demands and still make music of them, they pack an undeniable wallop.

I feel they are the summit of Strauss' operatic achievement. Whether you agree or not, they do confront us with an interesting artistic idea — one that I alluded to earlier in these essays — the power of great art to make what is objectively ugly and repellent into something powerful and even beautiful. Here are two operas peopled almost entirely with wretched, demented, even psychotic people doing awful things to one another. The action in both is unrelievedly grim, the atmosphere filled with terror and hate. Yet such is the wondrous power of Strauss' music that he compels our attention from the first bar, makes us listen and even has us exclaiming much of the time "how beautiful!" There are stretches in these two operas that are not beautiful at all, by anyone's standard, but they compel our attention by the sheer power of their utterance.

The musical language of these two operas is extremely complex, taking us on occasion to the brink of atonality. When the occasion calls for it, Strauss has no hesitation in writing something truly ugly, as in the quarrel of the five Jews in Salome. Think for a minute, reader, if you were writing this opera, what sort of music would you create to portray five religious fanatics shouting and screaming at each other over fine points of their doctrine?

Strauss scored his biggest success, of course, with Der Rosenkavalier (The Rose-Bearer), an opera that I have great difficulty in writing about because I consider it grossly overrated. In its three and a half hours of music there might be 45 minutes of truly inspired work; the rest seems to me mere filler, note-spinning that covers gobs of music paper without really going anywhere. Meant as a lightweight counterpoise to the two shockers that had preceded it, the opera pays tribute to the Viennese waltz and to the bygone days of Vienna's imperial glory. For reasons that escape me, it is extremely popular; before you make up your own mind, be sure to hear it complete rather than relying merely on the various suites of concert excerpts ("waltz-sequences") that turn up on symphony programs fairly often.

The remainder of Strauss' operas are in and out of the repertory with varying degrees of frequency. Ariadne auf Naxos and Capriccio turn up fairly often, the latter a leisurely and charming work that spends two and a half hours discussing the eternal operatic question: Which is more important, words or music? Die Frau Ohne Schatten (The Woman Without a Shadow), a complex and heavy-handed fairy tale that hymns the virtues of childbearing and family life, can be heard now and then, as well as Arabella. Each of these pieces, as well as most of the others left unmentioned here, have transcendently beautiful moments that sit uneasily amid musical commonplaces.

Aside from the Four Last Songs, the oboe concerto

and the nostalgically lovely Metamorphosen there is not much of interest in Strauss' other orchestral works. He was, however, one of the great contributors to the literature of the German lied, and great singers everywhere sing his song, both with orchestra and with piano. I would recommend, among many, these in particular: the lovely Zueignung (Dedication), Allerseelen (All Soul's Day), the superb Staendchen (Serenade) and Morgen (Tomorrow), Caecilie and the showy Amor. In these miniature pieces Strauss seems able to express himself more concisely and with less of the kitchen sink mentality that makes such a hodgepodge of good and bad out of his work in the larger forms.

Strauss lived through both world wars, and it is, regrettably, necessary to discuss his attitude toward the Nazi regime. At first he accepted a responsible post in their cultural apparatus, but later fell into disfavor with them and became persona non grata, largely because he seemed more interested in furthering his own career than in promoting the Nazi interests. He got into big trouble, for instance, by continuing to work with a Jewish librettist, Stefan Zweig; he seemed unable to understand why this was dangerous not only for himself but for Zweig as well. He was an apolitical person whose main concern with the Second World War was its affect on his international royalties. The Second World War does also seem to have plunged him into something like despair. The beautiful Metamorphosen for 23 solo string players is, on one level, a lament for the destruction during the war of the Munich Opera House, where a number of his works had been premiered. Today, more than half a century later, the proximate cause seems less controversial, but we still have a truly lovely piece of music.

George Marek put it best in his 1967 Strauss biography: "Strauss was not a Nazi; he was not an anti-Nazi. He was one of those who let it happen."

There is a feeling that Strauss' creative powers declined over the last 30 years or so of his life, but like so many such glib assumptions, this one has lately been subjected to careful retesting and found wanting. Some of the later operas have been re-examined and upgraded on the critical scorecards. Works like Die Liebe der Danae, Die Aegyptische Helena and Daphne have been found to contain nuggets of real Straussian gold. Indeed, Strauss was a masterly writer for the voice, both in opera and in the lied. He especially loved the soprano voice and wrote ravishing things for it; conversely, he shortchanged tenors, a breed toward whom he had an aversion.

I feel, however, that Strauss' major accomplishment as a composer was his expansion of the expressive voice and power of the symphony orchestra. Building upon Wagner's achievement, he reared up some wondrous edifices of sound the like of which had never before been heard. Nor was this merely a matter of pictorial realism; it had to do rather with the mixing and blending of orchestral colors, expansion of the orchestra's harmonic vocabulary and extension of the capabilities of individual solo instruments. If he had only been more self-critical in putting together those vast orchestral pieces, he might have stood even higher than he does today.

There is also in his work a disturbing vein of self-centeredness. The "hero" of A Hero's Life is clearly Richard Strauss himself — a fact that is proved by his quoting, in the section entitled The Hero's Works of Peace, from a number of his own compositions (one wag suggested that this section's true title should be "Pieces of the Hero's Works"). In another instance, Strauss turned a rather embarrassing incident from his personal life (it concerns a misunderstanding between himself and his wife) into an opera (Intermezzo), the hero of which bears the transparent pseudonym of Robert Storch.

To the general public, however, all this is mere quibbling. People go and happily listen to Heldenleben, applauding it to the echo, turning to their neighbor and saying, "Why can't composers today write lovely things like that?" This wildly uneven work, of course, was condemned by the grandparents of those same listeners as the last word in incomprehensible modernism. Strauss himself had the last word in the famous section of that piece entitled The Hero's Enemies, an unmistakably spiteful musical portrait of Strauss' critics, full of snarling, mean, small-minded, carping wind instrument wailing. Taken objectively, it is indeed pretty ugly music, but it was Strauss, the masterful musical portraitist at work, and no one seemed to mind. Not many composers enjoy the privilege of thus mocking their enemies publicly.

X. CLAUDE DEBUSSY (1862-1918)

Debussy occupies an especially complex position in the history of music. He stands at the confluence of a number of artistic currents, influenced by all of them and in turn exerting influences of his own. As is the case with so many other composers, he was condemned as an avant-garde terrorist by the guardians of musical orthodoxy in his own day, only to be accepted (though not without a fight) by audiences of a later generation. Probably no single piece of music in this century aroused so much derision and ridicule as did Debussy's now-famous Prelude a l'apres-midi d'un faune (Prelude to the Afternoon of a Faun) when it was new in 1894. This short piece (about 12 minutes), gentle and languorous in mood as befits its title, was condemned as an incomprehensible jumble of dissonances by early audiences. Today's audiences, lulled by its familiar (perhaps even over-familiar) purling cadences can only wonder at this.

The first word that leaps to mind when Debussy's name is mentioned is inevitably "Impressionism" a term borrowed from painting and applied to a group of French composers of whom Debussy was the foremost. In painting, the term refers to a style that emphasizes subtle blends of color and a hazy, somewhat indefinite, image as opposed to sharply defined realistic images. The musical equivalent of this involves subtle blends of instrumental color, an avoidance of rigorous conventional musical form, often a leaning toward inspiration from literary or pictorial sources, and experiments in harmony that blur the distinction between consonance and dissonance. For the record, Debussy himself disliked the term "Impressionist," but he could not stop its spread through the musical world where it remains firmly attached, limpet-like, to his name today.

Debussy also came along just at the flood-tide of Wagnerian influence in music, and after an initial attraction to the Wagnerian aesthetic, he set himself up as a kind of antithesis to it. He wrote only one opera — a strange and seductive work that seeks to deny and contradict the Wagnerian aesthetic at almost every point. Pelleas et Melisande is one of those works of art that stands uniquely by itself, a true original. It has never attracted a mass following among opera-goers, but there are enough people who cherish it to keep it from disappearing over the operatic horizon for good. Even those who end up dismissing it must first come to terms with it. It is not a work for the singer-groupie crowd, but it has other and subtler attractions.

Another influence that chance threw in Debussy's

way was that of Oriental music, whose harmonic structure and general aesthetic influenced him a great deal.

Like Richard Strauss, Debussy was a transitional composer who led music across the gulf from the late Romantic era into modern times, but whereas the bridge that Strauss built is a massive, commanding edifice of brick and steel that leads straight onto the main highway of the modern era, Debussy's fanciful structure of dreams and moonshine deposits us in a shifting, uncertain landscape without map or compass. It's a beautiful place, to be sure, but we don't quite know where we are.

Besides his single path-breaking opera, Debussy's main contributions to music were in orchestral music — ballets, extended orchestral pieces and the like — and in the field of piano music, where he has long been recognized as one of the truly great innovators of musical history. His output of chamber music is small but worthwhile, and he also wrote a good number of exquisite songs that demonstrate his style and technique brilliantly in miniature. His music in general largely neglects the classic procedures of symphonic "development," in favor of a continuous flowing musical line, often related to a text or to a literary or pictorial idea.

His modus operandi is nicely illustrated by one of his most popular extended orchestral works, the three-movement tone-poem La Mer (The Sea). It would be interesting some time to gather together an audience that had never heard this piece, or even known that such a piece existed, play it for them without revealing the title, and then ask them what if any visual images the music conjures up. I have a feeling that the answers would vary widely, yet once you know what the source of Debussy's inspiration was, the piece becomes a piece of musico-photographic realism almost worthy of Richard Strauss himself.

We hear in this music the calls of sea birds, the steady pull of undertow, the choppy motion of storm-whipped waves, the flat calm of a windless ocean expanse — any and every sea-mood you can think of. It is utterly impossible for me at least (born and raised on the seashore) to hear this music without calling up a whole series of sea images. There are melodies aplenty scattered through all three movements, but what is important about the piece is its play of orchestral color and its subtle variations in rhythm and texture — not the way themes are combined and developed as they would be in a Beethoven symphony.

The question that remains is this: Divorced from its pictorial associations, does La Mer remain a beautiful and satisfying piece of music? Of course it does. Its purely musical values are of a high order, though for their period they were somewhat unconventional. If this work existed only under the title Three Pieces for Orchestra it would still be one of the greatest achievements of its time.

A good deal of Debussy's other orchestral music remains in the active repertory, L'apres-midi d'un faune, the famous Nocturnes and the Spanish-flavored Iberia being some of the best-known examples. In all of these pieces Debussy's subtle handling of orchestral resources and his harmonic adventurousness are at least as interesting as the purely melodic aspects of the music, but this does not mean that these pieces are to be listened to as mere dreamlike background music. There is a tendency in some quarters to think of "impressionistic" music as vague mood-painting, hazy, indistinct and devoid of musical spine. Even some performers approach Debussy in this frame of mind, and it is usually to the disadvantage of their performances, for this is music which will repay the closest and most attentive listening, despite its lack of much of the formal structural apparatus found in mainstream Classical-era pieces.

Among Debussy's relatively small catalogue of chamber music, the G minor string quartet, op. 10, one of the earliest works displaying the hallmarks of his mature impressionist style, is the most considerable. It was his only venture into the quartet medium.

The truly remarkable opera Pelleas et Melisande, being a work for the stage, must be approached from a different angle. Debussy here sought to create a new type of opera, one that abandoned what he considered to be Wagnerian overstatement and excess in favor of a more fluid, subtle, understated approach based on the natural rise and fall of the spoken and sung French language. The orchestra is a kind of mirror, reflecting words and dramatic situations, but not generally seeking to embellish or overemphasize them.

The libretto is an only slightly abbreviated version of a symbolist play by Maurice Maeterlinck, in which the characters seem to lack wills of their own; they are rather tossed about like playthings in the hands of blind forces of Fate that they do not understand.

There is not a whole lot of outward stage action, and much of the action that we do see is ambiguous. Who is Melisande, anyway? How did the impetuous Golaud come to marry her so quickly after finding her weeping in the depths of the forest, unable (or unwilling) to explain herself? Someone has tabulated that Melisande tells seventeen palpable lies in the course of the opera. The whole opera is a kind of dream-play and Debussy's beautiful music conveys some of the aura of a mysterious not-quite-real vision being enacted before us. The construction of the libretto in a series of short scenes gives Debussy's orchestra the opportunity to pour out eloquent commentary during the intervals that link scene to scene.

The opera's whole score glows with a strange, unearthly beauty. I am reminded of a remark made by one of my college professors concerning a line in a poem by William Blake: "What does this mean," an undergraduate had demanded testily. "I don't know," the professor replied candidly, "but it sure is beautiful, isn't it!"

Pelleas will never be a popular opera, though it is showing some signs of relatively increased popularity these days. It offers no opportunities for singers to show off their high notes or their technical agility. There are no real arias in it from first note to last, with the arguable exception of the little ditty sung by Melisande at the start of the tower scene (act three in the printed score). The vocal line is for the most part recitative, with many whole phrases sung to a single pitch, and the whole line rising and falling in conformity with the flow of the French language. Do not let that idea frighten you, however; sometimes this sort of thing can be incredibly beautiful and expressive, as in the short scene in the first act where Genevieve reads aloud Golaud's letter announcing his return with his mysterious bride.

Pelleas is an opera of haunting, fugitive whispers and ambiguous suggestiveness. It is one of the most original and important works of twentieth-century music — and it does grow on you as you begin to grasp its gloomy and wraith-like loveliness. A few sketches survive (and have been recorded) for a second Debussy opera, based on Poe's Fall of the House of Usher, a subject certainly gloomy enough to be potentially congenial to the composer of Pelleas.

On the evening of April 12, 1945, the day on which President Franklin D. Roosevelt died, I attended a performance of Pelleas. The opera's air of subdued, understated gloom seemed to fit exactly the mood of shock that one felt in the arriving audience on that historic night.

But if Pelleas, for all its historical importance, is fated to remain a rarity in our concert life, Debussy's large and incredibly important output of piano music is not. These pieces, in which Debussy said he had unlocked the latest discoveries in "harmonic chemistry," are played a good deal, and have been recorded by some of the best pianists. The best way to get to know them, of course, is to play them yourself; but failing that, seek them out on recital programs or, as a last resort, haunt the record shops.

Debussy's piano music has suffered a fate common to a good many composers, the pieces that have attained the greatest popularity are by no means characteristic of his mature style. The two early Arabesques, the little Reverie and the ubiquitous Claire de Lune are perfectly good pieces of music, but they do not represent Debussy at his most "Debussyian." For that you have to look into his Images, the two books of preludes, the Children's Corner, the Estampes and the etudes. The riches that you will find there are extraordinary.

Many of the qualities that make this music both unique and attractive are summed up in a piece like La Cathedrale Engloutie (The Sunken Cathedral) from the first book of preludes. The title is suggestive of an old Breton legend about a cathedral that emerges once a year from beneath the sea, bells tolling and monks chanting. The music begins in mist, but gradually takes firmer shape and in the middle section we hear Debussy's very personal version of pealing cathedral-organ music and tolling bells; then the whole vision recedes once again into the mist. This music demands certain very special skills from the performer if it is to make its effect, notably expert chord-balancing and pedal technique.

Chord-balancing simply means that each note in a complex chord be given equal weight. Pedal technique in Debussy's piano music, with its delicate wash of constantly shifting sonorities, is a whole study unto itself. The pianist must avoid clashes that produce a harmonic hash while at the same time letting each passing harmony achieve its due resonance.

Other items in Debussy's piano output that will reward the careful listener might include the delicate Reflets dans l'eau (Reflections in the Water) and the scintillating Poissons d'or (Goldfish) from the Images, all three pieces in the fanciful Estampes, the wistful little waltz entitled Le Plus que Lent (a well-nigh untranslatable title), the justly celebrated Golliwog's Cakewalk from Children's Corner, in which Debussy showed both his fascination for American ragtime and his good-natured disrespect for Wagner; and perhaps the showy L'isle Joyeuse (The Happy Isle), a piece that proves there is a virtuoso-showpiece side to Debussy. In most cases the virtuoso display element, when present in his music, is kept strictly in the service of a poetic or pictorial idea, but in this instance it is given free rein.

It is worth mentioning, too, that while the titles of Debussy's preludes are suggestive and helpful to both listener and performer, in most cases they were added to the manuscripts only after the music had been written.

Debussy's output of songs also contains a number of fine pieces, but, like the piano music, it cannot be listened to as you would listen to Beethoven or Schubert. It is another animal altogether, and a peculiarly French one at that. The vocal writing may seem at first hearing to be mere recitative in the Pelleas manner. Many of the texts are full of rich, even overripe, romantic imagery and Debussy's intent seems to have been to clothe them in a kind of sensuous mantle of sound that will enhance their effect without obscuring the words. In a way it is a French response to the same dilemma tackled by Wagner in his operas, but where Wagner would thunder grandly, Debussy whispers seductively. The piano parts are beautifully written and in many cases take on an importance greater than that of the vocal line.

I think that Debussy's song La Chevalure (Tresses) from the Chansons de Bilitis, sung by the right singer, can be one of the most purely sensuous experiences in all music. Also appealing are Beau Soir (Lovely Evening), the vigorous Mandoline and the beautiful Il Pleure dans mon Coeur (It Rains in My Heart). One early vocal piece by Debussy, Lia's air from his cantata L'enfant Prodigue (The Prodigal Son) has achieved a measure of deserved popularity as a concert piece. It is important, though, for the listener to approach this music with the right sort of expectations. Fancy virtuoso chirping and foursquare tunes are not what it is about.

The Impressionist movement began in France and it is today commonly thought of in connection with

French composers, notably Debussy and Ravel. But it is important to realize that it also made some impact on the rest of the musical world. English-born Frederick Delius (who lived much of his life in France) was strongly influenced by it, and it produced a remarkable composer in America, the tragically short-lived Charles Tomlinson Griffes. Impressionism was not, however, fated to blossom into a permanent stream in the history of music parallel and equal to the central European mainstream. It blossomed relatively briefly, and then was swallowed up in the many and various other trends that came to be regarded as "modern" music in the middle years of this century. It survived, but not robustly. Perhaps it was too closely tied to the art and literature of a single country to become a truly international movement. Nonetheless, it produced two master composers and a respectable list of others who made notable contributions; the legacy it left is a permanent part of our musical life.

XI. ANTONIN DVORAK (1841-1904)

Dvorak's life and reputation bear some superficial similarities to those of Mendelssohn. He was an uncomplicated man, much loved and appreciated in his lifetime, a man of warmth and good nature, helpful to his fellow composers and deeply respected by his peers (Brahms was an especially close personal friend). His life, like Mendelssohn's, contained few serious personal crises of the sort that might draw from him deeply tragic music. He had an advantage over Mendelssohn in only one important respect — longevity.

While such generalities are always dangerous, one is tempted to say that the parallels between the two composers extend to their basically optimistic music. There are certainly moments of dramatic tension in Dvorak, but they do not seem expressive of deep inner turmoil of the Beethoven or Mahler sort.

In addition to the basic technical equipment and musical outlook of his time and place, Dvorak harbored within himself two other influences that shaped his music — a deep religious faith and the influence of the folk-tradition of his native Bohemia. Virtually all of his major works reflect his ethnic roots — his country's folk dances and folk songs, legends, and countryside.

This is true, I would argue, even in the famous New World Symphony, written on United States soil and, by Dvorak's own say-so, influenced by American folklore. In a famous magazine article written during his two-year stay in this country, Dvorak urged American composers to find inspiration in the folklore and folk music of American blacks and American indians rather than trying to imitate the sound and style of European models. Parts of the New World Symphony, he said, were music originally conceived for a cantata on the subject of Hiawatha. He minimized the idea, then prevalent, that the symphony was deeply influenced by the music of American blacks.

Yet if you listen to this piece afresh (if such a thing is possible after all these years and all these thousands of performances!), it seems to me that the interior landscape of this deservedly popular symphony is really Bohemian after all, rather than specifically American. Perhaps the second theme of the famous largo movement (the theme marked un poco piu mosso, a little livelier, for flute and oboe in mid-movement) might be thought to convey some suggestion of American Indian music, but it could just as well be a tune of European origin. The same can be said of the jaunty little opening subject of the third movement. Many have remarked on the resemblance of the first movement's principal theme to the spiritual Swing Low, Sweet Chariot, but it too could just as easily have been written under the influence of the Bohemian countryside. And it is hardly necessary at this late date to point out again that the famous English horn solo theme in the largo was original with Dvorak; it was only outfitted with a text (Goin' Home) and transmuted into a spiritual after the fact.

Dvorak suffered the same fate as Tchaikovsky, in that three of his later symphonies have become so popular that they have all but crowded out of our concert halls the six that preceded them. The later Dvorak symphonies in D minor, G major and E minor are indeed splendid works, fully deserving of their long-standing popularity; but it is unjust to concentrate so fully on them that the earlier symphonies, especially those in E flat and F, should be practically unknown to concertgoers.

The immense, and, to repeat, fully justified popularity of the three late Dvorak symphonies has had one bothersome side effect. When European orchestras visit our shores, especially those from Dvorak's home territory, they all seem to think that the ultimate compliment to an American audience is yet another performance of one of these symphonies, most often the New World but also frequently the G major or the D minor. Much as concertgoers love and enjoy these works, would it not be more stimulating for a visiting orchestra to play some less familiar piece from its own turf, whether a new work by a contemporary composer, or some piece from the past that we are not likely to know here? It is a chance to broaden our musical horizons that is too often left unrealized.

Dvorak has also suffered neglect, at least in the United States, in the field of opera. Only one of his nine operas, the fairy-tale Rusalka, has had any sort of career in this country (and not much of a career at that). It was introduced into the repertory of the Metropolitan Opera only in the 1993-94 season (92 years after its premiere) with high hopes, but, for whatever reason, did not draw well and vanished from sight quickly, like the water sprite Rusalka herself (it did reappear briefly at the Met, for just three performances, late in the 1996-97 season). I do not understand this at all, for Rusalka is a lovely score, with stretches of delicious water-music (its trio of sprites sometimes recalling Wagner's Rhinemaidens), some fetching dance music and several beautiful moments for Rusalka herself, notably her famous apostrophe to the moon.

A number of Dvorak's other operas are at least available in records, and those records give promise that full productions would reveal them to be stageworthy.

Dvorak's great strength as a composer was his wonderful (and seemingly inexhaustible) vein of delightful melody. All of his music sings. If there is a single piece that can be said to show this quality of his music at its most beguiling, it might be the lovely third movement (allegretto grazioso) of the great G major symphony.

Dvorak was less successful in matters of form,

tending to let his pieces sprawl a little and go on for a while after they have said all that they really have to say. This is another of those consideration that bother critics and musicologists no end, but which are of no account whatever with the general public. There is a good deal of padding, for example, in one of his most popular works, the famous cello concerto, but cellists go on playing it, and the public goes on listening raptly to it nonetheless.

The folk influence pervades almost everything Dvorak wrote, but it is most palpable in pieces like his two delightful sets of Slavonic Dances, written originally for piano duet but far better known to us in orchestral dress. These immediately appealing pieces, it should be emphasized, are original works, not Dvorak's symphonic versions of real folk-tunes. They stand more or less halfway between music actually intended for real dancers and the sort of idealized meta-dance music that Chopin gives us in his masterly but undanceable waltzes, polonaises and mazurkas.

There is something about the very term "dance music" that makes some concertgoers wrinkle up their noses in distaste, but virtually all the great composers from Bach to the present day have found inspiration in dance music, and the best of them have recast it in their own image in ways that enrich our concert-going experience. In these Slavonic Dances Dvorak seems simply to want his audiences to breathe something of the fresh country air of his homeland. Individual pieces from the two sets are frequently used as curtain raisers or fillers on concert programs and on records; actually the sets deserve to be heard in their entirety, as major items on such programs. Either one of the two groups of eight dances would make an excellent half of almost any concert program.

Dvorak's chamber music is equally attractive and it has attained an honored place in our concert halls and on records. The famous American string quartet (op. 96) is the best known single piece, but there are two other beautiful quartets, a piano quintet (op. 81), the lovely string quintet in E flat (op. 97) and the famous Dumky Trio (op. 90), among other pieces that ought to be in the ears of serious listeners. There are also quite a few pieces in smaller forms (e.g., the beautiful Bagatelles, op. 47 and the Biblical Songs) that are worth knowing.

Dvorak wrote a fair amount of choral-orchestral music. One superb example that comes around occasionally is his lovely Stabat Mater, whose most appealing section for me is the smoothly flowing section on the text Tui nati vulnerasti.

The beautiful but somewhat sprawling cello concerto has a firm hold on standard-repertory status, first because it is indeed a beautiful piece, and secondly because of the lack of a large repertory of really first-rate concerti for that instrument. Dvorak's violin concerto is also a splendid piece that for reasons unfathomable to me is not so well known as it might be. His piano concerto is not quite on a par with the other two concerti.

Because his life was comparatively undramatic and his music carries an immediate appeal, there has been a tendency to consign Dvorak to the second rank of great composers. It is true that he did not wrestle with Beethovenian demons, but, as is the case with Mendelssohn, it is not necessary to bare one's soul on music paper in order to write music worthy of being preserved in the repertory.

Except for the ubiquitous New World Symphony and an occasional short piece like the famous Humoresque, Dvorak's music has not duplicated the feat of Tchaikovsky's by becoming well known to a public that does not go to concerts. Perhaps the reason lies in the stark contrast between the lives of the two men — Dvorak's mostly serene and untroubled, Tchaikovsky's continually wracked with pain and personal crisis. Dvorak's life would never appeal to Hollywood. How could you make a movie about a composer whose consuming hobby was an interest in trains?

Nonetheless, I feel that Dvorak's music ranks with Tchaikovsky's in terms of its appeal to the beginning music lover. Tchaikovsky's public breast-beating strikes a responsive chord in people, but so too does the cheerful good nature and flowing melody of Dvorak. He makes an excellent introduction to the whole field of "classical" concert music.

Dvorak was a devout Catholic and much of his music reflects the serenity that comes from strongly held religious faith. This is certainly evident in every bar of the Stabat Mater mentioned above. There are also a Mass, a Requiem, a Te Deum and various other works on religious texts. I do not find a lot of strictly religious feeling in the symphonies and chamber music on which his reputation chiefly rests these days, but perhaps there is something at work beneath the surface there. These pieces reflect a basically optimistic world-view — God's in his Heaven, all's right with the world — which may well have its roots in religious conviction.

Anton Bruckner was also a devout practicing Catholic and his big symphonies have often, and I think justly, been called "cathedrals in sound." You can detect a feeling of religious grandeur, of apocalyptic thought and feeling in them, even without words or overt religious stipulations of any kind (though he did indeed dedicate one of his symphonies "to the dear God"). All those grand proclamations by the massed Bruckner brasses are surely "sermons without words."

No one would compare Dvorak's symphonies to cathedrals. He has come out of the church after Mass and gone rambling off through the Bohemian countryside, watching the peasants dancing, listening to the brooks, and contemplating the mountains. But the message he heard in church still lingers; it gives some of that buoyancy to his step, that lilt to his melody.

The folk influence on Dvorak's music has already been noted. Like many Europeans (most especially like Tchaikovsky) he suffered pangs of homesickness when away from his homeland for any great length of time. That was the motivation behind his stay in a small community in Iowa during his sojourn in the United States in 1892-95. He wanted to be around people who spoke his language and shared his ethnic heritage, so it was arranged for him to go off to the small Iowa town of Spillville, where he spent a happy summer and composed a good deal.

This raises, of course, the whole sticky issue of "nationalism" in music — what effect a composer's preoccupation with nationalist expression may have on his ultimate standing in the history books. It is a subject on which much critical ink has been expended.

Few if any of the very greatest composers, the top-ranked speakers in the musical parliament, were "nationalists" and nothing else. Mozart, Beethoven, Brahms, Bach, Wagner and company transcended nationalism. Their appeal is universal. They spoke to everyone. By and large those composers primarily considered nationalists occupy a secondary rank of parliamentary benches. They are right honorable fellows, but they do not rank with the top echelon.

Dvorak was certainly a "nationalist" in the way he exploited the rhythms, dance forms and melodic inflections of Czech (specifically Bohemian) musical life; but I think it would be a mistake to simply stuff him into the nationalist pigeonhole along with composers like Grieg, Albeniz or Khachaturian. His appeal, whether you ascribe it in any degree to religious feeling or not, is more universal than theirs. It travels more widely and more successfully. To extend the previous comparison of Dvorak with Tchaikovsky, both men had something more to offer than the sometimes constricting nationalist outlook. So too, for instance, did Chopin, a composer rightly regarded by Poles as the musical voice of their country, but also a composer who speaks to us all.

The comparison, too, of Dvorak with Mendelssohn may also yield some insights here. Mendelssohn was not a "nationalist" at all; he was a cultured cosmopolitan who happened to be German. The "local color" in pieces like his Scotch and Italian symphonies is of the picture-postcard variety, something sent home from his travels, not something felt in his bones. Dvorak had Bohemia in his very marrow; he could not help it.

Dvorak's music has been relatively impervious to the ups and downs of fashion over the years. He remains indestructibly popular and his cause has been materially aided by a corps of famous conductors and instrumental soloists from his homeland who have brought his music to every corner of the musical world. I recall a performance of the D minor symphony by the touring Czech Philharmonic under the late Karel Ancerl that practically set the concert hall ablaze with its fiery brilliance. Another virtue of his orchestral music is that much of it is almost conductor-proof; even a routine performance can still charm and delight an audience. It is solidly, often brilliantly, orchestrated, and once a conductor learns how to make its often rambling structure hold together coherently, success is within his grasp.

Dvorak was very prolific, and he is fortunate that a representative sampling of his large output is still heard by concertgoers, at chamber music evenings and solo recitals as well as in symphony concerts. Only in the opera house has he failed to achieve quite the status that he deserves. He has also been well served by the recording companies, which have atoned for their piling up of a Matterhorn of repetitive recordings of the last three symphonies by also dutifully exploring and preserving a good number of his lesser-known pieces as well. He is proof that good things can and do happen to lovable people, even in the melodramatic world of the arts.

INTERLUDE III: Pros and Cons About Recordings

It is safe to say that more people get their classical music "fix" these days through recordings than through all the other available media combined — i.e., live concerts, radio broadcasts, telecasts, whatever else you can name. The variety of repertory available in a well-stocked classical record shop can be staggering. The recordings pour out in a seemingly unstoppable torrent. And they sell (though lately the sales figures have flattened out somewhat and an air of crisis has enveloped the record industry, caused, in my view, by the sheer volume of "product" that is out there).

There is also no question that recordings have since the earliest years of this century been a mighty factor in spreading the classical gospel. They have clearly redrawn the musical map in all sorts of important ways.

I feel, though, that recordings are a two-edged sword. There are plus factors and minus factors. Used properly, they can contribute greatly to a musical education; used improperly or to excess they can greatly retard it.

First, the good news.

One major boon conferred on music lovers by recordings has already been alluded to — the vast expansion of the available repertory. We have available to us on CDs today a range of repertory utterly beyond the wildest dreams of past generations.

It may be hard for a younger person raised in the LP and CD eras to imagine a time when the only Mahler symphonies familiar to most listeners were the first, the fourth and, perhaps, the fifth, simply because these were the only ones among the Mahler nine that were short enough to be available on records. Now that Mahler has become an integral part of the standard concert repertory, recordings of his symphonies — even the more recondite ones like the sixth and seventh, not to mention the mammoth eighth — blossom like apples on an apple tree.

As reported earlier, I have long felt that the arrival of Mahler into the inner circle of the standard repertory in the late 1940s was a direct result of the invention at that time of the long-playing record. Prior to that time most of the Mahler symphonies were unknown quantities to music lovers because they were too long to fit conveniently on 78-rpm records. Back in the late 1930s there did appear, as previously mentioned, that 22-side recording on "78s" of the second symphony, but it never gained much popular exposure. Even when it was new, it was a sort of museum curiosity. Nowadays, of course, we even lack the equipment to play it on. What few copies still exist are the musical equivalent of dinosaur fossils.

The LP format suddenly made such works easily available, people began listening to them, and Mahler had arrived! Without downgrading the importance of advocacy by star conductors like Leonard Bernstein, I think the new record format was an equally important catalyst.

Composers who used to be mainly names in music history texts suddenly spring to life as their music is made increasingly available on records. There is really no excuse today for someone who professes a genuine passion for music not to be acquainted with a very wide spectrum of music, going far beyond Virgil Thomson's famous "fifty-piece standard repertory" list. It's all out there and available, much of it on library shelves for no-cost borrowing.

This is a gigantic plus for the music lover.

Secondly, recordings form an invaluable historical resource because they preserve — for a considerable time if not indeed for all time – a treasury of great performances. They make available a wonderful variety of interpretations by performers great, near great and not so great, that form an incomparable archive. They make possible all sorts of comparisons between performers in given pieces. Just imagine how valuable it would have been to have a recording of Beethoven as soloist in one of his piano concertos or of Bach at the Thomaskirche organ! In some cases, of course, today's recorded "performances" are not really performances at all, but versions spliced together in short "takes" over a long session in the recording studio. That said, however, I do not think it invalidates the recorded document as a snapshot of how a given performer or group approached a certain work at a certain time.

Chalk up another huge plus for the value of recordings.

And as a practical matter, it is certainly true that recordings bring music to a lot of people who have no access, either because of where they live or their financial status, to live concerts. This is a major factor in favor of recordings.

In many cases, this dissemination of music results from the airing of recordings over radio stations that specialize in classical music and reach into remote areas far from concert halls or opera houses. But the records had to be there first, before the radio folks could air them! The status of "classical music radio" has undergone fundamental changes in the last decade or so, mostly for the worse, but there is no denying the major role it has played in catching the ears of a lot of people living far from major musical centers.

I am not generally a fan of those ancient "historical" recordings made under primitive conditions early in the recording era. I know that they can often give us a reasonable idea of how some great turn-of-the-century singer, pianist or violinist approached music, but it seems to me that the sonic quality of these discs is often so primitive that there must often be a real question as to how much one can rely on them as true sound-pictures of their subjects. With a respectful nod to their historic importance, I cannot really recommend them for today's beginning listener, except as fascinating curiosities. Only later in one's aural education can they perhaps take on a stimulating but somewhat limited role.

Now pray consider the downside of recordings.

A recording, first of all, is always and inevitably the same thing every time you play it, something that can never be true of the live performance. The recording never changes. It is frozen, immutable, an immobile statue, not a living human entity. Listening to it is a one-way musical experience; you press the "Play" button on the CD player, and out the piece comes, as it has every other time you have pressed that button. There is none of the two-way electricity between performer and listener that so energizes the live-performance situation (if you doubt the existence of this phenomenon, just talk to any solo performer, conductor or orchestral player.) There is none of the suspense that goes with listening as a great performer comes to grips "live" with the extraordinary technical demands of the Hammerklavier sonata or Norma's Casta diva and tries to make genuine music instead of merely coping with extraordinary technical problems posed by the composer.

A corollary to this is that the recording almost unconsciously says to its listener: "This is the way this piece should go." If we live for a long time, as many people do, with one recorded version of a given work, we tend to feel that "this is how it goes," and any other interpretation, to the extent that it is different, is somehow "wrong."

The listening ear and the mind are gradually dulled to the idea of differing interpretations, to the truthful notion that there is no one single "correct" way to interpret any given work.

The truth, of course, is that musical notation is a very inexact science. There is no way that a composer can put down on score paper every single nuance that goes into the performance of his piece. In the early years, up until about the time of Beethoven, most composers did not really try. The scores of Mozart are very sparing in their dynamic and tempo indications. Some Bach scores, and those of many of his high Baroque contemporaries, even lack tempo indications altogether. One of the most painstaking of all composers in trying to put down on paper every detail that his performers might need was Gustav Mahler, the very same Gustav Mahler who also said, "the most important part of music is not in the notes."

I have another quite personal grudge against recordings in general: they make listening to music too easy. The record industry even touts this as a merchandising ploy: "Sit in the comfort of your own home and enjoy the majesty of Wagner, the elegance of Schubert, etc., etc."

What ever happened to the idea that listening to music should be something very special? That the listener should put something of himself into the process? That it should be an occasion? There is something to be said for the need to dress up, to travel to a concert hall, pay for your ticket and listen to great music in the company of a large gathering of kindred souls, each of whom is receiving the musical stimulus in his/her own way. We tend to value the experience, and hence the music, more if we must put some effort into it.

The record merchandisers are right, of course. It is so much easier just to sit at home, put the CD into the player, press a button and get your Stravinsky or Verdi effortlessly. But it also makes us value the experience and the music less than if we had to exert ourselves a little for it.

Most people who love classical music can point to at least a few friends whose experience of music comes almost entirely from recordings. Such folk tend to have at least a nodding acquaintance with a very wide repertory indeed, and they can rattle on endlessly about how sopranos A, B, C, X, Y and Z differ in their interpretations of Un bel di from Madama Butterfly. They will tell you that they actually prefer recordings to the live concert experience — a startling example of mistaking shadow for substance in my book.

The brilliant but eccentric pianist Glenn Gould made the superiority of recordings over the live concert experience a central article of his musical faith, and he gathered unto himself a considerable following who echoed that idea. I feel frankly that they were all totally, tragically mistaken. The precise opposite is true.

Such people, no matter how vast their knowledge of recordings, are missing something essential to the whole musical experience -- the human element. There is a hoary (perhaps even apocryphal) story about the young record nut who was finally dragged, kicking and screaming, to a live concert by the Philadelphia Orchestra and came away complaining that the band was "lacking in high frequencies." There's something missing in such a person's musical makeup.

There are even people who pride themselves on the sheer accumulation of records, seemingly whether or not they actually listen to them! I think it was the conductor Michael Tilson Thomas who wrote disapprovingly somewhere about the person who, when asked if he knows the Beethoven symphonies, replies impatiently "Know them? I own them! There they are, right up there on my shelf, see?" The records become visual trophies that announce to all comers "What a cultured fellow I am!" rather than music to be experienced and taken to the heart.

I once heard an opera lover boast that he had on his shelves twelve different complete recordings of Tosca. I wondered silently "Why? When can he possibly sit down and listen to them all? What is the point of such a piling up of duplications?" Certainly there are differences of interpretation among those twelve versions, but I wondered how often their owner took the time to do comparative listening.

Another species very much at large in the musical forests is the "sound nut," the person who is more interested in sound for its own sake than in music. He listens to the last few minutes of the first act of Wagner's Tristan mainly so he can savor the seven cymbal crashes that occur in it. His conversation is a thick gumbo of technical jargon rather than a discussion of music. When gathered in groups such people argue passionately the merits of speakers, amplifiers and other gadgetry rather than the merits of music, or even the merits of performers. They are certainly creations of the recordings era, but I don't think they can be called genuine music lovers.

So where does all this pro-ing and con-ing leave us? With a very valuable tool, but one that must be used with considerable caution if it is not to turn on its master like the legendary sorcerer's apprentice. It can be used to broaden one's knowledge of the repertory to any degree, subject only to the whim of the individual. And it can serve as both historical archive and introductory medium for someone unable to get to live concerts. Beyond that lie treacherous aesthetic quicksands.

To me, the first of those three functions is the most useful and important, but it is probably, alas, the one of least interest to most music lovers. Every audience survey and popularity poll reveals an overwhelming thirst on the part of the concertgoing public — for what? For endless repetitions of the "fifty piece standard repertory." There is very little spirit of adventure and exploration out there, at least by comparison. Symphony orchestra managements know that the all-Beethoven evening is a sure way to sell out the house — and the major record companies are not far behind in their willingness to pile up yet more versions of favorite standard works. Check your Schwann Catalogue listings under Beethoven and Tchaikovsky for confirmation. It is a matter of economics — of purveying to the public what it will pay to hear because that's what it likes.

To the beginning classical music fan, this can be useful. The pieces that form the backbone of the repertory are easily available in multiple versions by fine performers on major labels. But once you get beyond that stage, the search for recordings of lesser-known pieces can lead you into a confusing jungle of small labels that may not be so easily obtained. Problems of distribution and marketing that plague the record industry today are immense, especially for the smaller, more adventurous labels — and they do affect what you find in the store racks. There is even a growing body of opinion in the industry that identifies its chief problem (in a phrase I used above) as "too much product," too many firms spewing out too many CDs and thus splitting up the market so that few of them can expect to make any real profit.

So we must qualify to some extent our earlier tribute to the breadth of repertory that is available in the record shops. Once you start looking for Delius, Hummel or Koechlin instead of Beethoven, Brahms and Tchaikovsky, you will have a bit of a search on your hands. They all look very inviting in the pages of Schwann, but they are not nearly so easy to find on the racks.

Then, of course, when and if you reach the stage of taking an interest in genuinely avant-garde music, the search inevitably becomes exponentially harder. The labels get smaller, the number of copies pressed smaller too, the distribution system more rickety.

If I had a monthly budget for the purchase of records, I would split it in two and use half of it for tickets to live concerts instead. In some places, of course, that would not be practical; and the proportion of the split might even depend on what concerts were coming up that month. But the principle remains: one should use recordings for what they can do within their somewhat limited sphere of usefulness. Do not let them become a substitute for live music itself. Do not be like the apocryphal tourist who stood one day in Chartres Cathedral and exclaimed "Just think! Here I am in Chartres Cathedral! I can hardly wait to get home and see my slides!"

XII. GUISEPPE VERDI (1813-1901)

Opera was invented by Italians, and they have been its most assiduous practitioners for most of its 400-year history. The music history textbook generalization that says Italian music is basically vocally oriented while German music is mainly instrumentally oriented is reasonably accurate as textbook generalizations go.

Giuseppe Verdi was the most successful, and perhaps the most characteristic, of all Italian opera composers. Over a long career he produced about 29 operas (the exact total is arguable because two or three of them exist in substantially different versions that in one or two cases even bear different titles). They stand as landmarks not only along the career path of a single composer but along the broader path of the development of opera as an art form. A good half of them are part of the core repertory of opera houses today all over the world. People who would recoil in horror at the very idea of setting foot inside an opera house know La donna e mobile, the Anvil Chorus and Celeste Aida.

Verdi did what all truly great and innovative artists do. He took an art form from his predecessors, mastered its rules and procedures, and then proceeded to change them, finally passing on to his own successors an art form substantially different from the one he had received. When Verdi finished transforming Italian opera it was an incomparably deeper, more subtle, more psychologically probing and dramatically truthful thing than it had been before he touched it.

What he started with was the old Italian bel canto tradition, enshrined in a succession of beautiful and tuneful operas by Rossini, Bellini, Donizetti and other composers. These works, still widely popular today, were singers' operas pure and simple. Their primary purpose was to provide appropriate vehicles for great voices and great vocal techniques. They told stories, certainly, but the stories existed mainly as occasions for stringing together the musical numbers that served the voices. They were, and still are, beautiful works that deserve their popularity; but they were in general not deeply felt and shattering works of art.

Very early in his career — as early as Nabuco, his third opera — Verdi was accused of tampering with this tradition. His vocal and orchestral writing was accused of being crude, vulgar, noisy. He was put down as a sensation-monger, a man out to shock audiences, not to beguile or entertain them. The almost unrelieved gloom and bloodthirstiness of the plots he chose to set did not help his reputation either.

But it is important to realize that even as he deepened and energized the Italian operatic tradition, Verdi never really lost sight of the bel canto idea. Even in the great works of his maturity it can be found in those long, arching, vaulting melodic lines and in the sheer songfulness of many a solo scene. The difference is that it is there not as the be-all and end-all of the work, but as one musical component among a whole arsenal of techniques for clothing a drama in music.

The most popular of all Verdi's operas are the trio of great works from the early 1850s, Rigoletto, La Traviata and Il Trovatore. They represent the creative flood tide of his "middle" period, and they richly merit their immense worldwide popularity. They are not yet the vastly sophisticated and subtle musical creations of Verdi's last operas, Aida, Otello and Falstaff, but they show a deepening of the bel canto tradition achieved by wedding it to greater dramatic truth and a far more sophisticated use of the orchestra than was achieved by earlier composers in that genre.

Rigoletto, the 16th opera in Verdi's output, is the earliest of his works that has entered the worldwide standard repertory to stay. For a century and more it was assumed that his earlier operas, though containing many fine and beautiful individual things, were simply not worthy of being staged any more.

But then something curious happened. It started with the record industry's insatiable appetite for unhackneyed repertory — or, as they say in the trade, "new product." Record producers began looking into these early scores and they began gradually to find their way onto discs. Reviewers took note and public curiosity was whetted. As a result, four or five of these operas have advanced to the fringes of the everyday repertory: Nabuco, I Lombardi, Ernani, Macbeth, Luisa Miller. Others have also been heard sporadically in their entirety, and the whole canon has at least been recorded. And lo, a whole treasure trove of previously ignored music has been revealed. A century's worth of self-assured punditry has been discredited.

What these early operas have in abundance is Verdi's wonderful gift for flowing, characterful melody, allied to an irresistible rhythmic vigor. The orchestration may be on the crude side in more melodramatic moments, but in every one of the five early operas named above you can point to moments of wonderfully subtle orchestral writing that would not be out of place in the more celebrated operas of Verdi's later years.

To take only the most obvious of many examples: consider the great chorus of exiled Hebrews, Va, pensiero sull'ali dorate from Nabuco. Nothing could be simpler — a single flowing melody over the most elementary kind of rocking orchestral accompaniment. Much of the chorus writing is in unison rather than in harmony. The orchestral part is restrained yet luminous and supportive of the chorus. And yet this piece goes straight to the heart of any sentient listener. It is deeply moving music, all the more moving for its very simplicity.

Nabuco also affords a good starting point for consideration of another great Verdian invention, the act-finale ensemble in which all the characters get to express their varying emotions in a complex climactic ensemble that brings down the curtain with a theatrical bang. The second act finale of Nabuco shows Verdi just beginning to work at this idea. He gets hold of a great, swinging tune (S'apprestan l'istanti d'un ira fatale) and in this still rather primitive instance, simply repeats it five or six times, with different characters and the chorus chiming in to build a sense of cumulative drama.

Verdi worked at this in his succeeding operas with increasing skill and sophistication. The ensemble at the close of the third scene of Traviata and the convent scene ensemble in Trovatore show it in a much more advanced, but still not fully perfected state. It reached its Verdian zenith in four great later ensembles — the council chamber scene in Simon Boccanegra, the auto-da-fe scene in Don Carlo, the famous triumphal scene in Aida (best known of them all) and the incomparable third act of Otello.

These ensembles are masterly combinations of sheer threatricality, musical mastery and psychological rightness. In each case they advance the plots, they bring an audience to its feet and they are both beautiful and complex purely as musical compositions. Verdi was a man of the theater all his life. He did not look down on the idea of pleasing the public or making the box office a busy place ("the theater was meant to be full, not empty"). Yet it is wrong to classify him as a mere panderer to public taste, especially after he became famous and (eventually) wealthy. In Traviata, for example, he experimented with an intimate domestic drama, quite a different thing from the massive spear-and-sandal spectacles of the day, as exemplified in several of his own earlier operas. The very intimacy of Traviata contributed to the flat failure of its premiere.

In Rigoletto he had experimented, too, with a sordid story about a pack of really unattractive people, including a baritone title character who was shown to be as unattractive as anyone else onstage, but who evolved over the evening into a pathetic, tender, wronged man who enlisted the audience's sympathy. Verdi was criticized here for making an opera by dipping into a cesspool of moral corruption.

The opera also provided one example among many in Verdi's career, of his talent for getting into trouble with censors, both political and ecclesiastical, who had control over stage presentations in those days in Italy. The opera was based on a Victor Hugo play about the licentious King Francis I of France, but the censors were nervous about such open mocking of a monarch, so the king was demoted to become the Duke of Mantua instead.

What matters to modern-day audiences, of course, is not that sort of thing, but the increasing sophistication of Verdi's musical speech as his career progressed. Scene after scene proclaimed the arrival on the world operatic stage of a composer full of ideas and originality, a man who could raise opera to new heights of musical and dramatic truth.

Some of these scenes are so familiar to us today through constant repetition that we no longer hear them as revolutionary. A couple of examples: the nervous, scurrying, obsessive orchestral underpinning for the card-playing scene at Flora Bervoix's party in Traviata is something quite extraordinary in Verdi's output; and the wonderfully sinister low-string writing for the first meeting between Rigoletto and the professional murderer Sparafucile in Rigoletto is also something unprecedented, not only in Verdi, but in the whole spectrum of Italian opera up to that time. Compare the latter, for example, to the witches' choruses in his own earlier Macbeth ; the poor witches come off sounding like strays from some Gilbert and Sullivan operetta.

Four of the five operas that Verdi composed between Traviata and Aida are very much part of the standard opera repertory today — Ballo in Maschera, Forza del Destino, Simon Boccanegra and Don Carlo. Only I Vespri Siciliani is not a true repertory item, though it too turns up from time to time. Of this quintet I would nominate Boccanegra and Don Carlo as masterworks of the first rank, with Ballo very close to them but perhaps not quite on their exalted level. Forza seems to me a decidedly flawed piece whose best pages (the convent scene in particular) are the equal of anything in any of these middle period operas; but Forza suffers from its sprawling, episodic structure and from a considerable acreage of substandard musical inspiration (most of its military scenes). Boccanegra is a good example of a work in which superbly sustained musical inspiration triumphs over a convoluted and confusing plot and a general atmosphere of oppressive gloom. There is not a dull or uninspired number in it from first curtain to last. It presents a forbidding exterior to the listener who may not know it, but its interior is richly furnished indeed. Don Carlo also gives off an air of almost oppressive grandeur only occasionally leavened by lightness, but it is also a musical treasure house. Both works have only in recent years begun to establish themselves close to the center of the standard repertory; both obviously deserve that placement.

Aida presents a problem to the commentator by its very familiarity. By most reckonings it is the world's most popular and most often performed opera. It is also a superbly constructed and musically sophisticated work that does not deserve to be classed merely as a succession of popular song hits. Opera audiences have a habit of listening merely from hit tune to hit tune, which does a disservice to almost any opera but most especially to Aida, which is full of telling subtle musical touches that can pass unnoticed by ears that are only listening for familiar tunes, or worse, merely for high notes.

A few examples: the wonderfully evocative orchestral introduction to the Nile scene; the superbly human reaction of priests and people when Radames asks freedom for the prisoners in the triumphal scene (the stern priests, in fortissimo octaves demand "death to the enemies of our country" while the people, pianissimo say only "pity for the poor unfortunates;") the brilliant characterization of Amneris, who is a proud princess most of the time, but has moments of genuine compassion and in the end evokes our sympathy as she grieves over the tomb of Radames; the pseudo-Egyptian music that permeates the whole score, just exotic enough to give it needed atmosphere but never extended enough to get in the way of the main operatic action.

Aida is indeed a great work — and one that deflates conclusively the silly notion that because something is very popular, it must necessarily be of inferior quality.

Verdi's two final operas, so utterly different from each other, take his art even beyond the level achieved in Aida and bring it to a state of sophistication and brilliance unparalleled for that era in operatic history. Otello is his tragic masterpiece, a work of searing emotional impact and tragic grandeur; Falstaff is a light-footed comedy that moves with dazzling speed, so dazzling in fact that many of its delicious moments can pass before a less-than-attentive ear realizes what it is hearing. Thus Otello, by the sheer force and beauty of Verdi's music has established itself in the standard repertory, but Falstaff even now remains an acquired taste, a special piece that even today has not yet found its mass public.

The only major non-operatic work of Verdi's that has established itself firmly in the standard repertory is the famous Requiem that he composed in memory of the great Italian novelist Alessandro Manzoni. When it was new in 1874 (between Aida and Otello, that is) it was criticized as being too "operatic" in style, but this objection has wisely been discarded as simply irrelevant and the work now enjoys a lusty career as a concert piece, which is, of course, what it was intended to be anyway. It is not really adapted to performances in churches as part of actual funeral services (few of the many requiems by great composers are.)

It is indeed a colorful and melodramatic work, with emphasis memorably and heavily laid on the terrors of death and judgment rather than on sentiments of consolation or religious preachments (Verdi, though nominally a Roman Catholic, had no use for clergy or for organized religion in general). Verdi could hardly have been expected to change his style, honed through a lifetime of composition for the opera stage, into something else for purposes of this requiem. He simply wrote what was in his gut, as all honest composers do.

Beyond the Requiem, one hears of the non-operatic Verdi only the lovely Four Sacred Pieces, a splendid choral work, and a workmanlike string quartet that Verdi wrote during the Aida period. He was entirely a man of the theater, a composer with only sketchy formal training but one who learned his craft by the doing rather than from textbooks. All the biographers tell us he was an unpretentious fellow who, after success made him able to do so, simply followed his own lights and cared not a fig for the intrigues and politics of the professional musical world. He was happier by far puttering around on his farm.

And when he died, a national hero, it is said that the crowd that followed his coffin through the streets of Milan burst spontaneously into that moving chorus from Nabuco — Va, pensiero sull'ali dorate.

The perfect tribute.

XIII. GIACOMO PUCCINI (1858-1924)

Imagine a college classroom or lecture hall filled with musicologists, professors, critics and other heavyweight musical scholars. Each is given a pad and pencil and told to make a list of the ten greatest composers of all time (not, please note, a list of ten favorite composers, which is not at all the same thing.)

It is a safe bet that Giacomo Puccini would end up with very few, if any, votes when those papers were tallied. He is an anomaly — a composer wildly and indestructibly popular with the general musical public all over the world, but one who enjoys virtually zero respect among the musical high priesthood. We have remarked the same phenomenon to a lesser degree in Verdi's case, but Puccini is an extreme example. Let me say right off the top that I feel this critical disdain for his music is utterly unjustified.

Puccini, like Verdi, was first and last a composer for the theater, which may be one reason for his low standing in academia. He wrote no symphonies or sonatas, no instrumental concertos, nothing that would establish his name on the programs of our symphony orchestras. And he never taught anywhere.

Aside from a fair number of youthful works that have not lasted, he wrote only operas. Of his early output only the Messa di Gloria and the little string orchestra piece Crisantemi are ever performed, and these extremely rarely. Furthermore, though he was deeply interested in the modernist musical currents of his day, and though this interest is reflected to some extent in his later operas, he was never an avant-garde pathbreaker of the Stravinsky/Schoenberg/Ives type.

So with a respectful bow to that room full of frowning musical gatekeepers, let us look at this extraordinarily successful opera composer.

There are 12 Puccini operas, of which ten are heard today with varying degrees of frequency on the world's opera stages, 60-plus years after their composer's death (and all 12 are available on records). This is an enviably high batting average, approached or equaled in the opera world only by Wagner. Three of Puccini's operas, La Boheme, Tosca and Madama Butterfly, are among the most popular of all operas anywhere, performed season after season on virtually every opera stage worthy of the name, to wildly enthusiastic and emotionally affected audiences. Another three, Manon Lescaut, Turandot and the one-acter Gianni Schicchi, are heard rather less often, but are still produced often enough to be very familiar fare to anyone who takes his opera seriously.

And productions of the other four works. the one-acters
Suor Angelica and Il Tabarro and the full-length operas
Girl of the Golden West and La Rondine come along
at somewhat longer intervals. Only Puccini's first two
operas, Le Villi and Edgar, would appear to be truly out
of the running in terms of popularity.

In virtually all of his "hit" operas Puccini wrote about
recognizable human beings in very human situations.
Not for him the gods, goddesses, giants, dwarfs, love
potions, curses, rainbow bridges and airborne warrior
maidens that populate the Wagnerian universe. The only
time Puccini ventured into anything remotely like that
— in Turandot — his work is an obvious caricature of
legendary China, not meant to be taken seriously other
than as an excuse for some exotic musical "background-
ing."

In purely operatic-dramatic terms, Puccini is famous
for his gallery of vulnerable females, stretching all the
way from Anna in Le Villi through Manon Lescaut, Mimi,
Butterfly, Tosca, Sister Angelica, Magda (in La Rondine)
and ending with pathetic little Liu, whose funeral music
in Turandot was the last music he completed before
his death. (Puccini came by his knowledge of women
naturally, for he was a womanizer all his life and became
embroiled in at least one sensational public scandal
which, though he was ultimately shown to be innocent,
established that image indelibly in the public mind.)

But more importantly, Puccini's musical style is
a blend of sensuously shaped melody, incredibly bril-

liant musico-theatrical instincts, subtle and beautiful orchestration, a harmonic vocabulary that made use of many of the devices and innovations of "modern" music but within a basically traditional musical language, and a masterly use of the power of musical recall, i.e., the bringing back at a crucial moment of music heard earlier, as a means of putting the dramatic situation into poignant musical perspective. There are recurrent "motives" in his scores, but they are not "leitmotives" (leading motives) in the classic Wagnerian sense and they are not employed in anything like the systematic way established by the Bayreuth genius.

Puccini was very conscious of the theatrical aspects of his operas. He drove his librettists absolutely crazy with his requests for rewrites, revisions and tiny changes (down to the level of single words). One of his operas, Manon Lescaut, had so many hands involved in shaping its text to Puccini's exacting standards that the libretto was published with no one's name listed as author.

From a purely musical standpoint his operas are fairly easy to cast. The vocal demands of Rodolfo, Pinkerton and Cavaradossi are nowhere near those required of Wagner's Siegfried or Parsifal, and do not require anything like the stylistic purity necessary for Mozart's Tamino or Idomeneo. What Puccini does require is performers who can engage an audience's sympathy through means both vocal and otherwise, especially in his female parts. These operas are surefire — it is very hard really to wreck one of them beyond repair if the performers are schooled professionals. Great singing is always a plus, of course, but we still weep when Mimi dies, even if she is only a decent singer.

The phrase "theatrical effectiveness" turned up a few paragraphs back, as it inevitably does in discussions of Puccini. Those who denigrate his work invariably write those words as a term of opprobrium, with a sneer practically visible on the page. But when you sit in the theater, under the spell of Puccini's sensuous music, you are viscerally affected by it every time. The sudden entrance of the villainous Scarpia in the first act of Tosca, the lightning-fast switch from bloodthirstiness to awestruck moon-gazing by the chorus in the opening act of Turandot, the romantic first entrance of Cio-Cio-San in Butterfly, the tragic entrance of Musetta in the last act of La Boheme — these are moments that are unforgettable on first encounter (provided they have been intelligently staged) and that continue to affect us at every repeat performance, because Puccini has "staged" them in his music with such consummate craft. After the first hearing, of course, you know what is about to happen, but that does not really lessen the musical impact.

There was a noticeable growth in Puccini's musical language as his career progressed. The difference in harmonic subtlety between Butterfly (1904) and Girl of the Golden West (1910) is considerable. The orchestra is larger, the harmonic palette much more varied and complex, the orchestration more colorful. Commentators have found the influence of Debussy in the atmospheric music that raises the curtain on Il Tabarro and of Moussorgsky at the opening of the last act of Girl of the Golden West, and not without justification. Turandot, of course, is a special case — a work in which the composer set out to paint a never-never land of pseudo-Oriental sensuousness, decadence, mystery and picture-postcard charm. Reality in the Boheme or Tosca sense is a long way off in Turandot, as we learn within the first six or eight bars of its music.

I do not mean to neglect or downplay the well-known charms and excellences of Boheme, Tosca and Butterfly, but I would like to bear witness here first to the virtues of several of the less-often-heard Puccini works. The one-act Tabarro, for instance, the first of the three works making up the Trittico trilogy, is a taut and suspenseful lowlife melodrama, full of wonderful music and precisely observed atmospheric touches. It deserves far more hearings than it gets; and La Rondine (The Swallow) which was Puccini's attempt to create something in the general vein of a Franz Lehar Viennese operetta (but in the full operatic format which was Puccini's native metier) is a work of fragile charm that also ought to be better known. And I think that Girl of the Golden West is a far better opera than many critics (even many sympathetic to Puccini) give it credit for being.

On the downside, I will confess that I have so far been unable to warm up very much to Suor Angelica, which seems to me to cross over, for once, the line between sentiment and sentimentality.

Well then, what about that indestructible trio, Boheme, Tosca and Butterfly, the Tinker-to-Evers-to-Chance of operadom and the bread and butter of opera companies everywhere? They are all up-front honestly emotional works whose rather cornball dramatic values are raised by the power of Puccini's music to the realm of genuine art. All three are full of soaring melodies and unbridled passions of the sort often derided (but secretly relished) as "operatic." But in each I find also wonderful subtleties of musical expression that contribute to their overall effect in ways of which many in the audience may not even be conscious.

Let me cite a single example. Toward the end of the second act of Tosca occurs the super-melodramatic scene in which the lecherous Scarpia proposes to grant Mario Cavaradossi a reprieve from execution on the condition that Tosca, the distraught heroine and Cavaradossi's beloved, will, as the more delicate plot summaries have it, "give herself to him." Tosca, ashamed but desperate to save her lover, agrees, and we have the scene in which Scarpia writes out the safe-conduct pass that supposedly will clear the way. Throughout this scene the careful listener will note a repeated phrase of only two notes (a rising minor third in technical terms) which punctuates the music for no evident reason. Something sinister is afoot in the orchestra, we know — but what?

The meaning of this becomes clear only in the third

act, when the firing squad appears to carry out the "mock" execution and Tosca learns too late that they used real bullets instead. Just as the soldiers level their rifles and fire, the orchestra shouts out that same two-note phrase fortissimo. It is a musical tag for Scarpia's deceptiveness, obviously. I imagine that not many attendees at your average Tosca performance pick up this musical cue, but it is there in the score, and perhaps at his third, fifth, tenth or twentieth Tosca a listener gets the point. From then on, it is there to be relished; that listener's involvement with the musical drama has been a little heightened, and perhaps his appreciation for Puccini's craft enhanced too. The only clue in the opera's text is Scarpia's sinister order to his underling that the mock-execution be carried out "just as we did in the case of Count Palmieri." Some Scarpias can make their intention plain by the way they inflect that line, and the one that follows it ("Do you understand well?") But the music tells its own tale of treachery.

The performance history of these three famous and popular operas is interesting. None of them was an unqualified success at its world premiere. The 1904 premiere of Butterfly, in fact, constitutes one of the great scandalous fiascos of operatic history (along with those of La Traviata, The Barber of Seville and the Paris version of Tannhauser – not bad company). When new in 1896, La Boheme was regarded as an experimental departure for Puccini from the style of full-throated Italianate melody that he had shown in Manon Lescaut three years before. Much of it was regarded as too "conversational," a kind of light sprinkling of music over everyday conversational commonplaces. It is easy to laugh at this sort of incomprehension today, now that this opera is firmly established in the very front rank of worldwide popularity; but the Italian critics of a century ago were operating according to what they perceived as the standards of their day for opera. They were not antagonistic, just puzzled and disappointed.

Later in his career, of course, when Puccini had become a wealthy and world-famous celebrity composer, each of his new operas was greeted with great fanfare and critical hosannas. The world premiere of Girl of the Golden West at the Metropolitan in New York in 1910 was a media event of spectacular proportions. Interestingly, the work did not stay in the front rank of popularity and is only now beginning to emerge from the shadows to which I feel it has been unjustly consigned.

Puccini's operas in general make an excellent port of entry into the operatic world for newcomers, young and old alike. They are short, highly dramatic and musically very appealing the first time around. They do not make the intellectual-musical demands of Wagner or call for the refined musical sophistication that alone plumbs the true depths of Mozart's operas. The operatic newcomer who approaches Puccini must learn, however, to disregard the sneers of the cognoscenti — sneers for which I feel there is no real justification. When it was time for me to take my own daughter to her first opera I chose Turandot for the beauty and color of its music and for the abundant life and action in its stage-pictures. I have never regretted that choice.

Tosca might well be the absolutely ideal first opera for a young listener of our day and age. It is full of violence — murder, execution, suicide, attempted seduction and rape; the villain is the chief of police (how contemporary!). All this, of course, is what young folks absorb all the time these days from television. They should feel right at home with it. But the most important consideration must always be the music and Tosca, despite what many say in derogation of it, is chock full of wonderful music, not just the famous arias, either, but many other passages from beginning to end of the score. I always relish the little tone-painting of a Roman dawn that opens the third act, for example, and the thunderously theatrical Te Deum and procession that ends the first act.

One interesting peculiarity of Puccini's output is that Scarpia, the evil police chief in Tosca is the only real out-and-out villain in any of the still-performed Puccini operas. Jack Rance in Girl of the Golden West is not really a villain, he's just a law officer trying to do his duty and with the bad luck to be odd-man-out in the game of love that fuels the plot; even Michele, the pipe-puffing heavy and eventual murderer in Il Tabarro, is not a true villain either; he truly loves his sluttish wife. If you do not believe that, listen again to the touching duet between them toward the end of the piece.

There is no villain at all in La Boheme, and Butterfly is a case in which the romantic tenor hero of the first act turns into the caddish ne'er-do-well of the third. Gianni Schicchi in the popular one-acter named after him, is a most endearing rogue, and surely Princess Turandot, for all her posturing as a man-hater, cannot be called a villainess when she melts at the end and falls into Prince Calaf's arms! I suppose Tigrana in the well-nigh-unknown early opera Edgar might qualify, but how many opera-goers know her from firsthand experience?

The critics have delivered their verdict on Puccini over the years; it is condescending when not actually hostile. It is also wrong. The man had a wonderful gift and no one need feel ashamed to enjoy it.

XIV. MODEST MOUSSORGSKY (1839-1881)

In discussing Tchaikovsky earlier in this book I referred to the two opposing ideological camps which so influenced the course of Russian musical history — the cosmopolitan, Western-influenced style exemplified in most minds by Tchaikovsky and the Rubinstein brothers, and the nationalists headed by Mily Balakirev.

It is now generally conceded that the most original talent in the nationalist group belonged to Moussorgsky. Among the members of the so-called "mighty handful" of Russian nationalist composers he is the one best known to concertgoers and opera-goers today (the other members of the "handful" were Balakirev, the group's guru; Nicolai Rimsky-Korsakoff, Alexander Borodin and Cesar Cui).

Of these five, Balakirev was the only one who was a thoroughly trained professional composer. Rimsky-Korsakoff began as a naval officer; Cui was, of all things, a professor of military fortifications; Borodin is to this day known in Russia fully as much for his work as a chemist as for his music; and Moussorgsky started out as a career man in the Imperial Guards regiment, later holding jobs in the ministry of communications and the forestry department. Of the quintet, Cui and Balakirev have pretty much disappeared from the repertory except for a few of their smaller and less consequential works; Borodin and Rimsky-Korsakoff are fairly well represented by major pieces, but Moussorgsky, though his output was comparatively small, is a much more commanding presence than any of the others.

His life was short (he died at 42) and chaotic. The major cause of his death was alcoholism. There is no more heart-rending or revealing portrait of any musician than the famous painting of Moussorgsky by his friend Ilya Repin, done just before the composer's death. The composer looks out at us vacantly, yet with a certain air of wildness, clearly a disturbed soul, a man staring blankly at something the rest of us do not want to contemplate.

Moussorgsky shared with the other members of the "mighty handful" a consciousness of sketchy formal training, but unlike Rimsky-Korsakoff, for example, he seems to have let this bother him almost to the point of immobilizing his creative instincts and making it difficult for him to carry projects through to completion.

Rimsky's autobiography, My Musical Life, is an invaluable source of information on the work of this important group of Russian composers as well as being an honest account of Rimsky's own career. In it he freely admits that when he was first offered a professorship at the St. Petersburg Conservatory he was taken aback because of his own lack of musical book-knowledge, and therefore inclined to turn the offer down. Persuaded by Balakirev to accept it, he cheerfully admits that he had to work hard at first to stay one step ahead of his students and resort to subterfuges to make them believe that he really knew more about the technical aspects of music than they did. But Rimsky was a fast learner and he eventually evolved into one of the most technically accomplished of Russian composers, especially in the field of orchestration. Ironically, it was Rimsky who took in hand a number of Moussorgsky's unfinished major pieces and prepared them in what he considered performable editions, thereby putting himself at the center of a musical controversy that has not quite died down even today.

The list of Moussorgsky's works that are likely to be heard today is very small, but it includes titles that are extremely popular (the piano suite Pictures at an Exhibition, the opera Boris Godounov, the orchestral tone-poem Night on Bald Mountain) as well as others that may be less frequently heard but are well worth anyone's attention (the great song-cycle Songs and Dances of Death and certain others of his songs).

Boris Godounov is important because it is the finest example of the school of Russian nationalist opera. It is a kind of historical pageant made up of episodic scenes that reflect an important era in Russian history, but, more importantly, give voice to a musical idiom uniquely Russian, drawing on the inflections of the Russian language itself for their vocal style and on the resources of Russian folk song as well as the grandiose pageantry of Russian history.

The history of the genesis, premiere and subsequent career of this great opera is extremely complicated. It existed at various times in five different versions, and such was the confusion of its manuscript when Moussorgsky died that Rimsky-Korsakoff took unto himself the job of making it into a performable opera by planing away its "crudities" and smoothing out its chaotic harmonies.

For many years the opera was known on the world's stages only in Rimsky's version. Rimsky had said plainly in his book that Moussorgsky's original was still there, and if at any future time the world wanted to go back to it and set aside his revision, it could do so. In the meantime several other composers, including Shostakovich, had a go at reorchestrating and generally tidying up what was assumed to be an unperformable torso of an opera. It was not until the 1960s, with that era's emphasis on "historical performance practice," that thought was given to looking seriously at Moussorgsky's original.

When this finally happened, the verdict was nearly unanimous, and rather surprising: Moussorgsky's score was found to be not only performable, but a vastly more original and daring piece of work than any of the revisions. It seemed that the composer had meant exactly what he had written down. His well-meaning friend Rimsky, metamorphosed from naval officer dilettante into learned conservatory pedant, had sanitized and "corrected" a striking and original work by making it conform to textbook rules instead of to the wildly imaginative vision of its creator.

The original version is now universally accepted as the way this opera should be heard. It remains, of course, a loose and episodic work, a string of discrete scenes rather than a tightly knit organism. The title role, for all its grandeur, is one of the shortest in all of opera; the "love interest" (added at the insistence of the St. Petersburg Opera administration after Moussorgsky had submitted the opera for their consideration) occupies only a single scene very loosely connected with the rest of the opera. And there is still some debate over the order of the two final scenes: Should the opera end with the powerfully melodramatic death of Boris before the horrified members of the Duma, or should it end with the plaintive lament of the simpleton in the Kromy Forest while the skies behind him redden with the fires of revolt?

Most productions today opt — correctly, I think — for the incomparably poignant and moving Kromy Forest ending. Even so, I regard Boris's death scene as one of the three or four most gripping such scenes in all opera. It is one of the few whose music can almost convince the listener that he is present at a real death.

For many years the progress of this opera on western

stages was impeded by the perceived need to translate it from Russian into usually Italian, or some other language more commonly available among singers. Only in fairly recent seasons has the Metropolitan Opera in New York, for example, done the work in Russian. There are many fine older recordings of excerpts from Boris in Italian, and no one would want to forego the chance to hear a great singer (Ezio Pinza, for example) sing this music on records in whatever language; but it is a work that gains a whole new dimension when heard with the wonderful sonic roll and crash of the Russian language added to its notes. Moussorgsky's vocal lines, as noted above, are indissolubly wedded to the cadences of that language, and something is lost when another tongue is substituted. A similar situation of more modern date involves the once again popular operas of the Czech master Leos Janacek. The case of the famous piano suite Pictures at an Exhibition is another example of poor Moussorgsky's not being entirely allowed to speak in his own musical voice. This work stands today very close to the absolute top of the classical-music hit parade; it is performed everywhere and all the time, but more often in an orchestral version than in Moussorgsky's original for solo piano. It was taken up by Maurice Ravel, justly renowned as one of the greatest orchestrators among composers, and transcribed with great resourcefulness for the full symphonic complement. You can hardly look through a season's programs of any orchestra anywhere without coming across Moussorgsky/Ravel. There are probably audience members out there who are not even aware that this familiar piece started out as a piano solo.

As if that were not enough, other composers have followed suit. There are probably eight or ten distinct orchestrations of this work by different hands on the market. One conductor summed up the situation by devising a version of the suite in which each individual number had been orchestrated by a different hand.

There is no question that the piano version — famously difficult in its own right — suggests orchestral sonorities. The proliferation of orchestral versions, however, and the incredible popularity of Ravel's version, have stimulated pianists in recent years to trot out the piano original more and more often. A piece that was once regarded as among the most fearsomely chancy for a pianist to attempt is being heard (and recorded) from more and more pianists. A two-year-old edition of the Schwann record catalogue lists an unbelievable 101 recorded versions of this piece in all its incarnations — piano solo, orchestral – even arrangements for organ, two pianos, guitar and brass ensemble. And that was how things stood two years ago!

All this tends to obscure the fact that these are wonderfully imaginative pieces in their own right — pictorially effective and endlessly stimulating to the listener's mind. They are suffering these days mainly from overexposure; perhaps what is needed is the remedy that George Bernard Shaw suggested as the best means of celebrating the Bicentennial of Mozart's birth a five-year ban on all performances, so we could come back to the music at the end of that time with fresh ears.

A lesser-known work by Moussorgsky that is an undeniable masterpiece is the song cycle Songs and Dances of Death. This is one of the most unrelievedly gloomy, nay, morbid, works in all of music, but in the hands of a committed interpreter it can be riveting. The fact that Moussorgsky would think of setting such death-haunted poetry to music tells you something about the state of the man's psyche; the fact that he did it so successfully tells you something more important about the extent of his genius. The same Schwann catalogue that lists 101 versions of Pictures at an Exhibition lists five of this wonderful work.

A number of Moussorgsky's other vocal works, the Sunless cycle and The Seminarist, are certainly worth looking into. His opera Khovanschina has been heard here and there and contains some superb music, but it is handicapped by a complex plot based on an obscure episode in Russian history that is not easily sorted out by western listeners. Another of his operas, The Fair at Sorochinsk, is available on records.

This is a slim body of work indeed on which to base a claim that Moussorgsky was indeed a great composer. But I think the claim is valid. Undisciplined and tragically flawed as he was personally and professionally, he had a raw, blazing talent that cannot be denied. For all his deficiencies, he was the major exemplar of the Russian nationalist school at its best.

He also exemplified the composer who overcame a lack of systematic formal musical training to make a vivid mark in the world. There have been a surprising number of these. Wagner and Verdi, to name two, were not terribly well schooled in the formal sense. Among more recent composers, Elgar and Poulenc come to mind.

It is fascinating that this can happen in such a technically complex field as music. You can understand that a practitioner without a lot of formal training might write a great play, poem or novel (consider all the controversy that still surrounds the true identity and background of William Shakespeare); there are many examples of imperfectly trained painters producing masterly work.

But music is a language that requires mastery of a whole body of abstract techniques that are not, like words or colors, the common property of most people. Mozart stands alone as one, who for some supernatural reason seems not to have really needed to study the art (though, of course, he did so). It is indeed possible to acquire a degree of musical mastery on one's own, and that Moussorgsky did triumphantly. A large part of his tragedy was that he was so very conscious of his lack of technique, and allowed that knowledge to weigh him down creatively.

Rimsky-Korsakoff accomplished the same feat of more-or-less self-education in music, but he had a more stable emotional temperament than poor alcoholic

Moussorgsky and he was able to acquire the necessary book learning to a greater degree — to become, in fact, a professor himself. He was a fine composer (he is present in the modern repertory to about the same extent as Moussorgsky if you just count pieces) but he lacked the sheer fiery talent and inner conviction that drove Moussorgsky to keep working despite his obvious problems. His was a more refined, but a lesser talent. His eventual emergence as the reviser-in-chief of Moussorgsky's work is one of music's great ironies.

Moussorgsky also exerted a considerable influence on other composers extending far into the 20th century — and not all of them Russians. This is a further testimony to the worth of his accomplishment. There is a certain affinity between Moussorgsky and Debussy, both in the daring of their harmonic innovations and in the way they wedded their vocal writing to the requirements of their native languages. You could argue that the ghost of Moussorgsky can be spied here and there in other unlikely places — listen, for example to the opening measures of the third act of Puccini's 1910 opera *Girl of the Golden West*, with its starkly economical yet wonderfully evocative depiction of the pre-dawn hours in the "great California forest" in gold rush days.

Russia had a historical-musical problem that stemmed simply from its location far to the East of the great central European musical hives that produced so much of the music that defines our concert life today. It was regarded as an exotic backwater, a semi-civilized land of mystery whose music lacked the benefits conferred on more centrally located lands by the conservatories of Berlin and Leipzig. When the Russian Oulibichev produced a book on Beethoven in 1857, one European critic dismissed him as "that Cossack."

Tchaikovsky and Moussorgsky, from their differing perspectives, contributed to solving that problem. Tchaikovsky by building a bridge to the west, Moussorgsky by insisting that Mother Russia had something unique and wonderful to say on its own terms and in its own language. Each man's achievement illuminates the other's.

XV. CHARLES IVES (1874-1954)

Ives is one of the strangest and most eccentric figures in all of musical history. He is also one of the most important, a composer who labored in almost total obscurity during practically his whole life, then was recognized only after his death as perhaps the greatest composer his country has ever produced.

For most of his life he was pretty much an avocational composer. His main source of income was the insurance business, in which he made a great deal of money, and in which even today his name is celebrated quite apart from his celebrity as a composer. Ives came from a quintessentially American family background in Connecticut. In his music, as in his life, he is truly the most American of all American composers. but he achieved this in his own quirky way, without regard for the conventional rules of music or of career building.

Ives has been stereotyped as a far-before-his-time radical modernist, a man who was experimenting with techniques of the musical avant-garde long before anyone else. Another common stereotype has him down as a kind of charming primitive, a Grandma Moses of music. Thus it is important to realize from the start that Charles Ives had a thorough musical education, first from his father and later at Yale under the respected Horatio Parker. He knew the rulebook thoroughly; he just chose to throw it away and make up his own rules.

Another circumstance that has slowed down public knowledge of Ives's music is the fact that at his death, his surviving manuscripts (stored in a Connecticut barn) constituted one of the great musical confusions of all time. Editors, musicologists and performers had to sort through an incredible disorganized heap of score paper in an effort to piece together what Ives had actually intended. This effort continues to some extent to this day. I will confess that as a working critic I was often haunted by the alarming notion that some of Ives's wilder pieces, the Putnam's Camp movement from Three Places in New England, or the famous second movement of the fourth symphony, might actually have been the result of incorrect correlation among the various scraps found in that barn. Not likely, but at least possible in some cases.

Ives' father had been a Union army bandmaster in the Civil War, and he infected his son with his own adventurous musical spirit. The numerous passages in Ives' music that play off conflicting keys and rhythms against each other with blithe disregard for both techni-cal difficulty and the human ear's capacity to absorb sound are the direct result of George Ives' experiments. His son certainly took George's ideas a lot farther than the elder Ives had ever imagined, however.

You could argue that Charles Ives was a parochial fellow. He traveled very little and his world-view was pretty much that of the settled New Englander; his music is "American" in a kind of celebratory, Fourth-of-July sense, yet it transcends its maker's parochialism. It has a strong universal appeal that stems from its very air of directness and openness. It puts on no cultured "airs" and does not pretend to be anything beyond what it plainly is.

Ives had an open contempt for rule-bound academics, and his favorite derogatory epithet for music he didn't like was "nice." His iconoclasm sometimes led him to write things that are patently impossible to play; he sometimes seems to be saying to the perspiring performer, "How are you supposed to do this? That's your problem."

He wrote a good deal for orchestra, including five works that bear the title "symphony" (though you have to stretch the meaning of that term rather a lot to cover them all), some of the most fascinating chamber music ever produced in this country, a lot of finger-cracking piano music, including the famous Concord sonata, and a wonderful series of songs that are still being explored by our more adventurous singers.

These diverse songs perhaps sum up Ives in a small compass. Some of them are parlor ballads of the sort that were popular in Ives' youth; but others are of the most extraordinary modernity, calling for singers and pianists who can make them work despite their unconventional style and technical difficulty. Dissonance abounds. Vocal lines are jagged in the extreme. Rhythm is bent and fractured.

A few of them (General William Booth Enters into Heaven, for example) have achieved some celebrity. Among the more arresting items in this extraordinary grab-bag of vocal music are the raucous Circus Band, the whimsically brief Ann Street, the partly atonal The Cage, the folksy The Greatest Man and the imaginative Charlie Rutlage. These songs are so diverse in their styles — marches, hymn-tunes, ballads, folksy ditties, complex art songs, even political pronouncements — that each listener must sort them out for himself.

In a preface to his famous self-published book of 114 songs Ives made a famous declaration: "I have not written a book at all. I have only cleaned house." The songs should be experienced in that spirit. Taken as a whole they are certainly not for everybody, and most especially not for those who seek only to be lulled by conventional tunes and soothing harmonies; but each listener will find something among all that bewildering, disorderly diversity, to make him sit up and take notice. This is certainly the most valuable collection of songs yet produced by any American composer.

Ives lived until 1954, but, dogged by ill health, he composed little or nothing over the last 30 years or so of

his life. Recognition came to him only late in life, after
he had for all practical purposes stopped composing.
Many of his pieces, large and small, had complicated
gestation histories extending over many years. He would
take a page or so from some piece he had written as a
young man and incorporate it, with whatever revisions
were necessary, into a much later piece for an entirely
different medium. Sorting all this out and determining
the exact pedigrees of some of his pieces has become
a scholarly industry whose work is not really finished
yet.

An important strand that runs through all his music
is the incorporation in it of the vernacular music of
his own time. Protestant hymns of the day are strewn
through his scores like raisins in a pudding, as are military
marches and even allusions to the classics (the famous
"Fate" motive from Beethoven's fifth symphony plays
a prominent part in the Concord sonata, for example).
What is fascinating, though, is that these tunes are
almost never quoted exactly; they are rather suggested,
hinted at, distorted. They are there, we recognize the
allusions, but Ives almost always stops short of literal
quotation.

This in fact brings up one of the major problems
listeners have with Ives today. Much of the vernacular
music that runs so integrally through his scores is no
longer part of our common musical speech. We no longer
recognize those allusions to hymn tunes because we no
longer know the originals — and so some of the point of

Ives' discourse is lost. It is sad that much of the impact of Ives' music thus becomes the property of the very people he so distrusted, the scholars, rather than reaching the plain folks among whom he liked to number himself. Today it is the academics that dig out the original tunes to which Ives made musical reference, and point out to us his ingenious use of them.

At the outset of this essay I referred to Ives as "perhaps the greatest composer his country has yet produced." I should like now to delete the "perhaps" from that sentence and nominate him for the top spot without any qualifying weasel words. If he had turned out to be merely a fine "American" composer, that would have been a worthy accomplishment, but it would not have been enough to make him our best. His music, in addition to its self-evident "American-ness" displays a freshness and originality along with a depth of deeply felt emotion and a sense of awareness of great philosophical currents that give it a much wider appeal.

Also attractive to me is the noncommercial character of Ives' achievement. He was not really writing for money, since he had plenty of that from his career in insurance. He felt no need to please anybody else, or to "write down" to some mythical mass public in search of instant acceptance. Like every other composer, of course, he wanted to be accepted, but it had to be on his own terms. He produced his thorny and difficult scores as though simply saying to the public "Here is something I want to say to you; I hope you like it — but if you don't, well, too bad..." There was, indeed, a streak of the stubborn Yankee in the man.

Before Ives became recognized for the unconventional genius that he was, America had been content with several generations of perfectly respectable composers, most of them trained in the great European conservatories, who wrote music that imitated the European mainstream. In my own youth the conventional wisdom had it that our very best was Edward MacDowell. Ives changed all that, once his reputation began to blossom. The music of these earlier Americans, people like Foote, Chadwick, Paine, and Ives' teacher at Yale, Horatio Parker, does not deserve to be forgotten. They wrote some fine things that still deserve to be heard, but their work pales beside the wild, undisciplined and utterly inimitable music of Charles Ives.

Much is made by musicologists of Ives as avant-garde innovator, experimenting with things like tone clusters and atonality long before more famous composers closer to the musical mainstream got those ideas. This may well be a true assessment of his work, but he did not himself seem greatly interested in such things. He was a musical "sport," an isolated phenomenon simply doing his thing without much reference to what was going on in the well-mannered mainstream of music out there beyond his horizons.

Among Ives' major orchestral music, the most often heard items are probably Three Places in New England and the second and fourth symphonies. Three Places is indeed a small masterpiece or, rather, three small masterpieces combined into a single work. The opening movement, inspired by a statue commemorating the deeds of colored soldiers in the Union army during the Civil War, has a slow, plodding motion to it, under which we hear the incessant beat of a military tattoo; the second movement is one of Ives' celebrated orchestral battlegrounds, in which tunes in different keys and rhythms contend noisily, with a fine disregard for the rules of harmony and counterpoint. The effect of this wild melange is accentuated by the sudden silences that interrupt its course every now and then. The piece grinds to a raucous halt, only to be succeeded by a wonderfully quiet and imaginative little tone-poem descriptive of the bucolic Housatonic River, a piece that somehow achieves through enormous complexity a feeling of utter restfulness.

The second symphony. much more conventional in its language, is probably a good place to start if you don't know Ives' music very well. Its five movements are brilliantly varied and beautiful, and the bumptious finale ends with the orchestra declaiming Columbia the Gem of the Ocean in Fourth-of-July-oratory style. The very last couple of bars are an Ives joke: the trumpets sound "reveille" and the last chord is a jarring dissonance, stuffed with all 12 notes of the chromatic scale at once.

The fourth symphony is a work of such complexity that it was long considered simply unperformable; but, as often happens with such pieces, it is now heard and has been recorded often enough to display its innate worth. Its uproarious second movement is an even more complex Ivesian melange of everything-at-once than the Putnam's Camp movement in Three Places.

There are also a number of shorter orchestral works by Ives that manage to suggest his unconventional musical philosophy in miniature fashion. The best known is the quirky Unanswered Question, an effort to make music carry some very heavy philosophical freight, indeed. The "question" is posed by a solo trumpet; a wind ensemble argues with itself over the proper answer, and a distant string ensemble plays soft, imperturbable, unchanging "music of the spheres," unmindful of the argument. The whole thing takes about six minutes. The much played Variations on America is an orchestration by William Schuman of a humorous piece Ives wrote for organ in his college days. It caused a good many raised eyebrows at Yale, and Ives hugely enjoyed his little joke.

Ives' piano music is full of the same sort of highly personal quirkiness that distinguishes the rest of his output. The famous Concord sonata, long considered unplayable, is at once a summing up of his musical personality and a tribute to the New England school of Transcendentalist philosophers with whom he identified. The Hawthorne movement has cracked the fingers of many an ambitious pianist.

There is another fascinating Ives piano sonata, modestly entitled Three-Page Sonata (though the score occupies ten pages or so, a typical Ives whimsy), and a number of other fascinating and utterly unconventional piano pieces with titles like The Gong on the Hook and Ladder, The Anti-Abolitionist Riots and Some Southpaw Pitching.

Ives' chamber music includes four splendid violin sonatas, a delightful piano trio and especially two string quartets, the second of which is a gem. It bears a typically Ivesian programmatic inscription about four friends who get together to talk and argue, then ultimately go outside to look up at the nearby mountain. This amounts to a nice blend of two sides of the Ives personality — the gregarious New England townsman and the mystic Transcendentalist.

Ives does not turn up on concert programs as often as he should. Even today, when he is universally recognized as a composer of worldwide significance, some performers are afraid to offer his unconventional pieces to conservative audiences. Ives would have understood this – he was used to being misunderstood and neglected in his own lifetime. He also would have held such audiences in contempt for their "sissy ears."

As is the case with many composers outside the musical mainstream, Ives has been well served on records by devoted performers who made his cause their own. First among equals in this honor roll is the pianist John Kirkpatrick who virtually single-handedly began the Ives Renaissance by rescuing the Concord sonata from obscurity and proving that a dedicated musician could make music out of it.

Charles Ives was one of the great originals of musical history. He absorbed the mainstream European tradition thoroughly in his college days, but from his father, from the ideas of Transcendentalism and from deep within himself he added something else, a streak of stubborn Yankee originality that led him down lonely and untrodden paths, paths that ultimately led nowhere, for he founded no "school," attracted no followers. He was indeed a whole "school" unto himself.

XVI. IGOR STRAVINSKY (1882-1971)

For some years in the 1940s, Igor Stravinsky and Arnold Schoenberg lived within a mile or so of each other in Los Angeles, rather like the Popes of two rival religions. They had met a few times over the preceding years, but their relationship during their American years has been aptly characterized as an "armed truce."

Rightly or wrongly the two composers were considered the heads of opposed musical camps — Schoenberg of those composers who followed the vastly influential "twelve-tone" composing methodology he himself had invented, and Stravinsky of those who chose to go in other directions.

The rivalry made good copy for musicological treatises and cocktail party chitchat among insiders, but for the general concertgoing public there was never any doubt as to which man was guardian of the One True Musical Faith. Stravinsky's music, not all of it to be sure, but a number of his representative major works, had long since become a staple of the concert-hall and recorded repertory; Schoenberg's music, though much celebrated and analyzed by his circle of adherents, has not even today gained real acceptance among concertgoers or record buyers.

Now, 50 years or so after Schoenberg's death and 25 or more after Stravinsky's, there is no question that both men rank among the most important composers of the twentieth century, but there is also no question that Stravinsky has made his mark through his music, while Schoenberg, rightly or wrongly, survives more as an influence on other composers than through performances of his own pieces.

Stravinsky's detractors — and he has had plenty of them over the years — call him a "chameleon" who changed his style to suit the shifting winds of musical trendiness. He was a pupil of Rimsky-Korsakoff, the famous Russian nationalist composer, and his earlier works, the ones on which his popular fame mainly rests today — show an interest in Russian folklore. The three vivid ballet scores by which he is mainly represented in concert halls and on records today all date from this period, The Firebird (1910), Petrouchka (1911) and The Rite of Spring (1913). Then at about the time of his Octet (1922), Stravinsky entered into a neoclassic stylistic period, in which he wrote many works echoing the styles and procedures of Baroque and Classical period composers, but in every case putting his own Stravinskyan stamp on the final product. In a few cases Stravinsky actually reworked (his own term was "recomposed") specific pieces by composers like Pergolesi (in Pulcinella) and Tchaikovsky (in Baiser de la Fee).

Then in the early 1950s Stravinsky underwent another, and rather more startling stylistic change — he began writing serial (twelve-tone) music in the system pioneered by Schoenberg, who had only recently died. These later works have not attained anything like the popularity enjoyed by the works of Stravinsky's two earlier creative periods, but one thing must be said for them in general — they do not sound like Schoenberg (or like Anton Webern, whose influence Stravinsky specifically cited). Stravinsky may have adopted the Schoenbergian technique, but what he did with it still bore a uniquely personal stamp, just as the works of his neoclassic period had done. Stravinsky may have changed his compositional style several times, but he continued to be a unique and always fascinating musical voice.

During the week of Stravinsky's death in 1971, it happened that Pierre Boulez was guest-conducting the Cleveland Orchestra, and on his program was the American premiere of one of his own substantial new pieces. Boulez graciously removed his own piece from the bill and substituted an in memoriam performance of the Firebird suite, a gesture which I felt reflected great personal credit on Boulez, a man often reproached with having no human feelings at all. (There was an ironic side to this affair too; Boulez as a young student in Paris just after World War 2 had organized and led a noisy protest demonstration at a concert which featured one of Stravinsky's smaller-scale pieces, the Four Norwegian Moods. Boulez was careful to explain afterwards that the students' unhappiness was not directed against Stravinsky himself or against that piece specifically, but rather against the whole idea of neoclassicism and the tendency of concert programmers to go for "safe" works rather than those on the cutting edge of modernism).

That program change also set me to thinking. Despite Stravinsky's long career, immense world fame and overwhelming musical influence, The Firebird was probably the only piece of his that any major orchestra could trot out on a couple of days notice and prepare for public performance. Even Petrouchka and most certainly The Rite of Spring cannot simply be whipped together hastily even by the best of orchestras.

The vivid color and exotic tunefulness of Firebird and the extroverted folksiness of Petrouchka have justifiably kept them in the repertory for these many years. But The Rite of Spring is something else again — a wrenching, grinding, dissonant bombshell of a piece that sweeps us away even today by its sheer sledgehammer power.

If we are unable to recapture the sense of avant-garde "newness" with which opening night audiences greeted Beethoven symphonies in their day, it is equally possible that we have by now heard The Rite so often that its incredible audacity and pounding rhythmic energy do not hit us as powerfully as they should. The story of the riot that it caused at its world premiere (as a staged ballet) is well known. Today, by contrast, The Rite always places in the top ten when classical music radio station conduct popularity polls among their listeners!

There may be hope, though. A couple of years ago I had occasion to play a recording of this famous piece for a group of high school students, none of whom knew it at all. One girl was honest enough to remark afterwards, "As far as I'm concerned, that's just a lot of ugly noise." Of course, she was right. It is "ugly noise." But it is also a work of incredible suggestive power and a kind of rude, craggy beauty. Like so much great music, it changes us as we listen to it.

The Rite is one of those pieces, like Wagner's Tristan, that changed music at a single stroke. Stravinsky's reliance on rhythm as the engine that drove his music was novel enough, but the fact that it was not regular rhythm was a further audacity that bewildered early audiences. In The Rite rhythm is constantly being fractured, thrown off the track, jarred and jostled about. There are passages in which Stravinsky sets up, for a time, a regular pulse, only to have it rudely shattered. The Ritual of the Ancestors section is a good example.

The use of dissonance and the reliance on wind and percussion instruments, with a corresponding de-emphasis on strings are other facets of this piece that shocked its first hearers. The timpani, for example, are all-important. Pierre Boulez once remarked that in the final Sacrificial Dance, where the time signature changes with virtually every bar and many accents fall on "weak" beats, his job as conductor amounts to "playing tennis with the timpanist."

The Rite is also a good test case for the commonly heard plaint that "modern music" has no melody. The piece is full of melody, but melody is not its main center of attraction. Ears that are put off by its free use of dissonance and its unorthodox orchestration may not hear its melodic richness at first, but it's there.

The Rite of Spring still sounds very "modern" indeed, though it was written over 80 years ago. Its triumphant entry into the standard repertory proves that there are other ways to compel concert audiences to listen beyond merely lulling them with sweet sounds.

A number of works, large and small, from Stravinsky's neoclassic period are heard quite frequently today, notably the Pulcinella and Baiser de la Fee suites and the brief but utterly fascinating Symphonies of Wind Instruments written in memory of Debussy. Several works of chamber music from this period are also very much with us in concert and on records. One splendid and frequently heard piece that predates this period is the dance-drama L'Histoire du Soldat (The Soldier's Tale), a piece for dancers and chamber ensemble that is often heard complete or in the form of a suite of excerpts.

Among major scores from that general period, two especially stand out — the "opera-oratorio" Oedipus Rex and the Symphony of Psalms, written for the 50th anniversary of the Boston Symphony Orchestra. Oedipus Rex is not often heard, but the Symphony of Psalms has rightly taken its place as a 20th-century classic. Both have a quality of stately monumentality and a kind of grand ceremonial seriousness that set them apart from many of Stravinsky's other works, which have more the air of occasional pieces. Stravinsky set the Oedipus story, based on Sophocles, in Latin as a means of enhancing its remote grandeur, but he was persuaded (somewhat reluctantly) to allow the use of a narrator who would recall the unfolding dramatic story to the audience (always in its own language) as the work progressed. The end product is a work of austere grandeur that deserves to be much better known than it is. The Symphony of Psalms, much easier to produce, has rightfully become a classic.

Stravinsky's neoclassic period reached its climax, and its end, with his only full-length opera, The Rake's Progress, premiered in Venice in 1951 and now heard quite frequently on the world's opera stages. This was neoclassicism with a vengeance, an opera in a clearly tonal and harmonically simplified idiom, with clearly defined arias, duets, recitatives and ensembles, done throughout in a musical style of pellucid clarity. Stravinsky's detractors had a field day with the piece, calling it "Mozart and Scarlatti with wrong notes," but the work quickly made the rounds of major houses, and has remained a presence on many stages for over 45 years. It also had the benefit of a libretto of genuine literary distinction from the pens of W. H. Auden and Chester Kallman, based on the famous series of etchings by William Hogarth.

The Rake is a most engaging and attractive piece. a sprightly moral tale told in a sort of flippant way, both as to music and words. Among its many attractive pages, one may cite especially the touching little serenade sung by Ann Trulove to poor daft Tom in the final scene ("Gently, Little boat").

Stravinsky's adoption of the twelve-tone method of composition took the musical world by total surprise. He had never before shown any great interest in it — had in fact denigrated it on several occasions. There was much talk of putative influence exerted over him by the young conductor Robert Craft who met him at about this time and became a close musical and personal associate for the rest of Stravinsky's life. Craft was an exponent of the twelve-tone (or "serial") method, especially as carried out in the works of Schoenberg's pupil, Anton Webern, and Stravinsky always claimed that his own interest in the system stemmed from admiration for Webern's works. This whole question of whether Craft influenced Stravinsky in the twelve-tone direction is one of those nine-day-wonder musical controversies that seems quaint only a generation after it took place with such sound and fury.

Even the most committed Stravinsky disciple would have to admit that the works of this final period in his career have not enjoyed much popular success (of course, whether "popular success" is the be-all and end-all of composing music is another matter altogether). Some of them have a kind of austere appeal that can win friends for them in committed performances, the Canticum Sacrum of 1955 and the later Threni and Requiem Canticles are cases in point. But the fact is that they simply do not receive enough performances to allow them to make their way into the public musical consciousness. They are almost all available on records, but remember that the record buyer must first make the decision to buy something before he can get to know it — and he is not likely to buy something he has not heard somewhere else first.

By the time of his death in 1971, Stravinsky was firmly established as one of the musical giants of the twentieth century. His career stretched back well over 65 years and he was as much of a household word as any living composer of "serious" music could become in this day and age. He had made major contributions to just about every form of concert music, with the possible exception of the "pure" (i.e., unvocal, non-programmatic) symphony. He remains a strong influence on music through younger composers who were attracted to his style and through the vigorous musical polemics in which he engaged in print, sometimes on his own and sometimes through the refracting lens of Robert Craft's pen.

We are still perhaps a little too close to his dominating presence to make any sort of final judgment. There is a saying in the music world that immediately after a composer's death his reputation is likely to go into eclipse for thirty years or so, and only after that period has elapsed can one hope to predict where his reputation will come to rest. From today's vantage point, it appears there has been no real downturn in Stravinsky's reputation as a whole. There has been something of a shakeout in the list of his works in terms of frequency of performance — some major pieces that were hailed with great huzzas when new are no longer commonly met with in concert; but the man's looming influence is as great as ever, and the three mighty early ballet scores are an immovable part of the standard concert repertory. Firebird and Petrouchka seem, in fact, like classics from a previous era of musical history, so comfortable have we become with them. The Rite of Spring remains a genuine phenomenon, a work of startling originality that was many years ahead of its time and still sounds avant-garde to honest ears, but that has somehow won the enthusiastic endorsement of a wide public.

Stravinsky's long life and prolific composing career have conferred upon him a very special status in the history of music in this century. His youthful links to Rimsky-Korsakoff and the Russian nationalist school place him in the context of a movement that stretches back very far into the 19th century. Yet he remained a central figure in music through two world wars and much of the unsettled postwar period, which gives him a very contemporary relevance also. He is a survivor; he covered a lot of musical ground, and very sure-footedly indeed.

On the morning after his death I was asked to write something about him for my newspaper. I felt I could do no better than to call his close friend, the late Dr. Victor Babin, who was then director of the Cleveland Institute of Music. Stravinsky had always enjoyed Babin's company, in part because he and Babin could speak Russian together. I made the call and Dr. Babin reminisced about the great composer for twenty minutes or more. I began to fear I was trespassing on his time, so I ended the conversation, hung up and began to write.

A few minutes later the phone rang again. It was Babin, with an afterthought. He wanted to relay something Stravinsky had said to him the very last time they were together. Dr. Babin wasn't at all sure what it meant, or even whether it could be accurately rendered into English, but he wanted to pass it on.

The great composer had looked at Babin and said enigmatically, "You know Babin — the hardest thing in life is to survive until death."

I have been pondering that line for a generation and I think I have an inkling of what Stravinsky may have meant in his gnomic way. He might have meant that as long as you draw breath you have an obligation to give your all to life, to live fully, deeply and actively

If that was indeed what Stravinsky meant, he had fulfilled his own prescription superbly well.

XVII. ARNOLD SCHOENBERG (1874-1951)

We deal here, as intimated in the previous chapter, with the fascinating and important question of the relative importance of influence and popularity in the musical universe. It is a question that goes far beyond the merits, or the lack thereof, of two famous composers; in fact it goes beyond composers as a group; it concerns performers and even critics.

There is no question that Arnold Schoenberg left a huge and indelible imprint on twentieth century music. His large school of pupils and followers has carried his banner forward into the musical fray for over forty years since his death. There have been ups and downs in his posthumous fortunes, but there has never been any question that he is a force to be reckoned with. I think it was the Italian composer Luigi Dallapiccola who wisely remarked that all young composers, no matter what their personal stylistic bent, should master the technique of the twelve-tone method "if only to be able to reject it intelligently."

Yet Schoenberg, with the exception of a single vastly untypical early piece, has never been beloved of concert audiences or of record buyers. His music is still more written about and analyzed than it is performed. The truth is, in fact, that his name on a concert program even today tends to depress ticket sales. That does not, however, nullify another fact: no one can really grasp the course of concert music in this century without knowing at least some of his major works.

Schoenberg's career, like Stravinsky's, went through a number of distinct stylistic periods. His early scores are much influenced by the late-romantic harmony of Wagner and Richard Strauss; then for a time he abandoned the idea of tonality (that is, music written in conventional keys), and finally in the early 1920s devised his own system to replace tonality, the famous "system of composition with twelve tones related only to one another" that has made his name famous (or infamous, depending on who is rendering judgment.)

One of his early works couched in the late-romantic style is the famous string sextet Verklaerte Nacht (Transfigured Night), a half-hour-long tone-poem that is perhaps more often heard in a version for full string orchestra. It is by far Schoenberg's most frequently heard piece — and it deserves to be heard, for it is indeed exceedingly beautiful and expressive. Any ears familiar with Tristan or with the later Strauss tone-poems will have no difficulty with this fervidly romantic score.

The next step beyond Verklaerte Nacht for listeners

might well be Schoenberg's second string quartet, a seminal piece in that one can almost hear the process of liberation from romanticism and the approach to new and uncharted musical terrain taking place before his ears in this music. Part of the problem that audiences today have with truly "new" music is simply that they try to make the leap all at once from, say, Mahler and Strauss (though for some to be sure, it goes further back, to Brahms and Schumann) to the most modern experimental pieces. It cannot be done, just as you cannot leap across a mile-wide river at one bound; you need stepping-stones, intermediate way stations where you can see both where you have been and where you are headed. Schoenberg's second quartet seems to me an ideal stepping-stone within his own output. It includes a soprano solo in the last movement, a setting of a poem by Stefan George that may provide a helpful sentiment: "I breathe the air of other planets..."

Some of Schoenberg's later and far thornier works only begin to disgorge some of their expressive secrets to the listener who comes to them with some knowledge of their place in the continuity of musical history. His somewhat lurid one-character opera Erwartung (Expectation) for instance may not sound beautiful or expressive to the opera-goer whose taste stops at La Boheme or La Traviata, but to one who knows Salome and Elektra, Schoenberg's piece falls into place as the next logical step beyond Strauss in harmonic complexity and orchestral ingenuity.

The one Schoenberg work (again, an early one) that perhaps merits increased public exposure more than any other is, alas, not likely to get it because of its sheer size. His great cantata Gurrelieder (Songs of Gurre), written in 1901 but not performed until 1913, shares with Mahler's eighth symphony the prize for reaching the outermost limits of romantic musical gigantism. It calls for several soloists, a large chorus, a "speaker" and an enormous orchestra to tell a picturesque mythic story of lost love. For the most part, the work's musical language is that of late romanticism. One of its sections, for solo contralto and orchestra, the Song of the Wood Dove, has had a fitful vogue as a separate concert piece; but toward the end of Gurrelieder comes something quite extraordinary and prophetic — a section called The Wild Ride of the Summer Wind for speaker and orchestra, in which Schoenberg's free rhythmic treatment of the spoken text and his wonderfully picturesque orchestration tell us that he is on the brink of new and highly experimental musical departures. The whole thing foreshadows the revolutionary union of music and song-speech that he was to achieve later in Pierrot Lunaire.

Whenever Gurrelieder does get performed, it sweeps audiences off their feet; but the apparatus it requires is enormous and costly – and the effort to coax audiences who do not know the piece to listen to it can be daunting, given the formidable reputation for complexity that attaches to Arnold Schoenberg's very name.

There are other early Schoenberg works, the some-

what turgid but still attractive orchestral tone-poem
Pelleas and Melisande is one, that might provide a means
of entry into his musical style for someone unfamiliar
with it. The important thing is that the process be a
gradual one.

This is not the place for a detailed exposition of
the rules of the twelve-tone system. Schoenberg did not
devise this method of composition, as some believe,
because he felt that the old key-centered system was
exhausted. He insisted, on the contrary, that there was
"still a lot to be said in C major" — and many subsequent
composers have proved him right. But he did feel that
the rules, implied or explicit, of the tonal system were
too constricting, that there was another language out
there waiting to be developed that might prove to have
equal expressive possibilities.

A key to his thinking was his expression "emancipa-
tion of the dissonance," which seems to have meant
simply that the old distinction between concord and
dissonance was abolished by Schoenbergian fiat. Nothing
henceforth was to be regarded as a dissonance and hence
inadmissible. The idea of "twelve tones related only to
one another" meant enforced musical democracy — any
chordal combination of those twelve tones was to be
permitted so long as it served the composer's expressive
purpose. (It should be noted here that the "twelve tones"
to which Schoenberg and his followers refer are simply
the twelve notes contained in a chromatic octave; play
any twelve adjacent notes on a piano, white and black

keys — and you have played a chromatic octave. What Schoenberg did away with was the notion that eight of these – the eight contained in the familiar do-re-mi-fa-sol-la-ti-do scale pattern — are the defining elements of the music's "key" and that the others are mere subsidiary "half-steps" there to provide chromatic variety. In his musical universe all are equal and there is no "key" pattern.)

Schoenberg's basic idea was to arrange these twelve "equal" tones in some predetermined order and without repetition as an underlying basis for whatever composition is in hand, then to use variations on that basic row as a further means of achieving variety — running it backwards, turning it upside-down (so that a given interval going up became the same interval in a downward direction) and then using the upside-down version backwards. In addition to these four basic permutations, each "row" could begin on any one of the twelve degrees of the scale, since what was important was not the note itself but the interval distance between it and the next note. This gave the twelve-tone composer a total of 48 different permutations of the basic "row" with which to build his piece. What he did with them from that point on was largely up to himself.

There is much more to Schoenberg's formulation than that, but that will do for a basic introductory summary. In a word, the "row" and its permutations were Schoenberg's alternative to the scales that are integral to the key-centered tonal system.

The important thing, and something that Schoenberg himself always emphasized, was that the technical process itself was NOT the important thing. What was important was the expressive result. He wrote in one of his letters that he longed for the day when people would leave concerts of his music "whistling the tunes." That day, alas, has not yet arrived.

Part of the continuing "Schoenberg problem" is that audiences have heard so much about the complexities of the twelve-tone system that this is what they tend to concentrate on when confronted with the music itself. Program notes and commentaries that accompany Schoenberg performances are likely to be festooned with formidable charts and diagrams and musical examples that look odd, whatever they may sound like when played. I am convinced that an audience that came, say, to Erwartung without any preconceptions based on knowledge of its twelve-tone process, would be much more drawn into its expressive world and captivated by its elusive beauty than an audience "prepared" in advance by chalk-talks from Schoenbergian experts.

A very special case indeed, and a work like almost no other in all music, is the 1912 song-cycle Pierrot Lunaire (variously translated as Moonstruck Pierrot or even Loony Pete), a work not in the twelve-tone system but simply atonal — that is, without any key-center. It is a cycle of 21 expressionist poems set for sprechstimme (speech-song) and a chamber group of five players playing a total of eight instruments. The sprechstimme technique, though perhaps not exactly invented by Schoenberg, was here adopted by him and carried to new heights of expressive possibility. Pierrot Lunaire remains the work in which it achieved its greatest visibility.

Schoenberg was aiming at a vocal expression halfway between song and speech. Pitches are indicated in the score but they are only to be hit fleetingly — the performer is instructed to immediately glide off from one pitch in the direction of the next. The result is a kind of crooning effect that in much of the piece attains an eerie expressivity that fits the wildly imaginative subject matter. At other times, or in the hands of a less-skilled interpreter, the whole thing can sound merely artificial. It is worth noting that the sprechstimme performer at the world premiere was not a singer but an actress, one Albertine Zehme. In my experience each performer who approaches the sprechstimme assignment in this piece does so in his or her own way — some are close to conventional singing, others to ordinary speech.

There is no doubt that on a first hearing the effect of Pierrot Lunaire is startling, even unsettling. Like many worthwhile things in art (and in life) it takes some getting used to (there was indeed a first-class riot at the world premiere; Schoenberg was forever after very proud of this). You have to learn to listen past the unusual idiom and into the expressive core of Schoenberg's music, which is rich indeed.

Among others of Schoenberg's works that will repay careful listening one might mention the contrapuntally rich Second Chamber Symphony of 1940, his relatively often heard Five Pieces for Orchestra (1909), the song-cycle Book of the Hanging Gardens (1908) and several of his groups of short piano solo pieces.

Schoenberg had a number of prominent pupils, the two most famous of whom were Alban Berg (1885-1935) and Anton Webern (1883-1945), both of whom came very close to eclipsing their master in terms of public acceptance. Berg, whose application of the twelve-tone method was less systematic than Schoenberg's, has contributed several pieces to the modern standard repertory, notably his magnificent violin concerto and the searingly beautiful opera Wozzeck.

Webern (who was accidentally shot to death by an American occupation-force soldier during a blackout in 1945) became, after his death, the father figure for an intense but short-lived movement in postwar avant-garde music — the school known as "post-Webern serialism," which looked to his aphoristic little pieces for inspiration but sought to extend the "serial" (twelve-tone) principal to other aspects of music besides pitches.

Even today, nearly half a century after his death, it is difficult to place Arnold Schoenberg in his final historical niche. If, as some say, he led music into a cul-de-sac, it certainly turned out to be a busy and productive cul-de-sac, one that produced a large body of influential and challenging music that cannot be dismissed as of no account.

There is undeniably a reaction against the Schoenberg aesthetic in progress today. It was doubtless fueled by the zealotry of some of his latter-day disciples who carried his theory to extremes and tended to cast aspersions on any fellow composer who did not follow their banner. There was a time when post-Webern serialism was the rigid received orthodoxy of American academia, and no faculty member who did not follow the "party line" had much hope of recognition as a composer by his peers.

All this has (happily) changed. A much ballyhooed "return to romanticism" has taken place, though how long lasting it will be is anyone's guess. The ranks of the doctrinaire Schoenbergians are thinned and scattered. The future of his twelve-tone system remains in doubt. But more important than that is the simple fact of the music itself. It is still with us and the best of it compels our attention. These are major works — perhaps written in a language that falls strangely on the Brahms-oriented ear, but still music with a lot to say. Sometimes it is well worth learning a foreign language in order to experience an Aeneid or a Divine Comedy in its original tongue, unfiltered through the mind of a translator.

Schoenberg did not help his own case by being, from the near-unanimous testimony of those who knew him, a prickly and difficult person who never suffered fools gladly and who regarded anyone who disagreed with his view of things as something of a personal enemy. The collection of his letters issued in 1965 by Saint Martin's Press bears out this view abundantly. But the historical roster of great composers is full of prickly and difficult characters who also happened to be transcendent geniuses whose music has enriched us all.

Whether Schoenberg is of that number has not yet been decided. The jury in his case has been out for an extraordinarily long time, so their deliberations must be hot and heavy indeed. One of the problems we listeners face is that we do not get enough exposure to the evidence to make up our own minds. In the final analysis, the verdict will not be rendered by cloistered musicological jurymen, but by the listening public.

INTERLUDE IV: The "Modern Music" Dilemma

No topic occupies the musical establishment (i.e., critics, administrators, educators and presenters) these days more than the question of how to develop an audience that will actually enjoy, and thus pay money to hear "modern music."

Many open-minded and sincere audience members wrestle with the same problem. Many such people sincerely want to develop a taste for newer music but continue instead to be baffled by it. A much larger percentage of the audience, however, simply refuses to listen to it.

First, a definition is needed. It makes no real sense any longer to complain about "twentieth century" music now that the twentieth century is over. Composers like Hindemith, Prokofieff and Stravinsky, once regarded as the last word in avant-garde radicalism, have passed safely over into the category of "modern classics." You can almost hear the sound of sculptors' chisels working on their marble busts to set beside those of Mozart and

Beethoven in the musical temple. It has thus become common by now to date the period of "difficult" modern music from mid-century, or perhaps from the end of the Second World War in 1945. For convenience's sake let us do the same — always with the proviso that the "modernity" of music can never be measured solely by the calendar. The Rite of Spring of 1913 still sounds incredibly modern, much more so than many a neoclassic or neo-romantic work written 75 years or more after it.

In the city where I live there is a superb museum dedicated to the celebration and display of old automobiles. They sit proudly on the showroom floor, polished to a fare-thee-well, seemingly ready to go out for a spin any time. They date from the 'teens and the 20s, on up through the 1950s and early 1960s.

They are in that museum because they are "antiques." Yet, much of the concert music written in those same years is considered by many listeners to be incomprehensibly "modern" — i.e. dissonant, arrhythmic, unmelodic, an affront to the ears.

How can this be? People would not think of wearing today clothes that were fashionable in 1870, living only in houses that date from that period, or reading only books that were a minimum of a century old; yet in the field of music, the old reigns supreme and the new is largely scorned. People who would not think of looking only at Rembrandts or patronizing only plays by Chekhov insist not on new music but on endless repetitions of Beethoven, Brahms and Tchaikovsky.

Part of the problem, I think, stems from the rapid proliferation of musical life, the easier availability of more and more music, over the past century or so. We have so much more music available to us to be heard and assimilated, that it is difficult to keep up with the flood. New styles, new technical advances come along almost on a weekly basis. Even the interested and conscientious listener cannot keep abreast of all this "new music."

It is not really possible to make the adjustment from comfortably familiar older masterworks to the cutting edge of the avant-garde in a single bound. You cannot cross a wide river in a single leap — you need stepping-stones so you can make the crossing one step at a time. The listener whose musical time clock stopped perhaps with Richard Strauss is obviously not able to connect directly with the music of Stockhausen. He has to make the connection gradually — after first being convinced somehow that it can be made at all.

We can perhaps start our investigation with Strauss himself. Most composers go through a stylistic evolution over the course of their composing careers, and Strauss was no exception. His earlier works (Aus Italien, Don Juan) do not sound like what came later in his life (Salome, Elektra), but they are nonetheless recognizably by the same person. A traceable evolution has taken place; a new, more complex and challenging style has evolved. The same could be said for Schoenberg – compare Verklaerte Nacht or Pelleas und Melisande with his thornier later works.

(In the case of Richard Strauss, it is important to note that toward the end of his long creative life he reverted back to a more "romantic" style in two late works that are among his finest, the lovely Metamorphosen for string ensemble and the wonderfully poignant Four Last Songs. Many composers change styles, often quite drastically, in the course of their careers. No one should be surprised at this and no one should hold it against them. Truly great composers are not concerned with such ephemera as "styles" and "trends;" they write what is in their guts — what they have to write.)

I have always felt that Schoenberg's second string quartet is a seminal work in modern music, because in this single work you can almost hear the old style being supplanted by the new. There are certain composers whose output in general seems to exhibit this same trait; I would name the superb Danish symphonist Carl Nielsen as a prime example, and Bela Bartok as another.

Another composer of that generation bears mentioning here, though he was more backward looking than he was progressive. I refer to Ernest Bloch, a man who scorned schools and fads with a withering contempt. He believed strongly that a composer must be true to himself and write only what is boiling around inside himself crying out to be liberated onto music paper, no matter what style it exemplifies. I have always respected Bloch for that honest attitude, and I dearly love his music. Composers like Nielsen, Bartok and Bloch are "bridges," ways of going from the safe "late-romantic" bank of the river out onto the first of a series of stepping-stones than can ultimately lead you to the distant "modern" bank.

What these composers were doing was challenging the accepted rules of what in their formative years constituted listenable music. Strauss in Salome and Elektra extended the bounds of harmony beyond Wagner. The allowable quotient of dissonance was raised, and the definition of what constituted a dissonance was liberalized. This process, of course, had been going on for several hundred years before Strauss. Listen to the first few bars of Beethoven's First Symphony, which was condemned as "dissonant" in its day. Remember that critics condemned Chopin's piano music for its "ear-splitting dissonances."

Rhythm, too was gradually being granted more freedom. The regular pulse that was the basis for so much earlier music was giving way to something much more varied, with more frequent changes of time signatures. Stravinsky was a prime mover in this department.

And of course there was the familiar complaint of "no melody" – a charge that has been leveled against innovative composers in every musical era. Composers did indeed adopt a much more liberal definition of what constitutes a "melody" — just as Beethoven had when he invented the famous four-note motto that forms the major musical substance for the entire first movement of his Fifth Symphony. Among the "bridge" composers under discussion, my favorite example of the new type of melody is the vaulting, leaping opening theme, the "hero" theme, that opens Strauss' Ein Heldenleben. You can't whistle it — the range is too great; rhythmically it is quite irregular; yet it is undeniably a "melody" – a striking and rememberable linear element that can be made part of the musical material of an extended work.

Composers operating since 1950 or so have extended these various musical boundaries even further. They have enlarged the orchestra itself, and found new connections between it and disciplines like the theater, dance and literature. They have even, in a few extreme instances, made us ponder the question of what exactly is music, and what is not. It has been a time of extraordinary musical fertility, with dozens of different styles and schools contending for the public's ear. The musical scene is full of both wild-eyed radicals and backward-looking conservatives.

Both listener and critic face this extraordinary variety of available new music and, in their bewilderment, begin looking for rules, for guideposts, for shortcuts to making sense of it all. There is always the temptation to anoint one favorite school or style as the in-music of the day and then simply to denigrate all others; a distressingly large percentage of our criticism goes that route. It is much harder, but infinitely more honest to try simply to distinguish good from bad, honest from insincere, competent from incompetent, emotionally cathartic from merely contrived, on a piece-by-piece basis without regard to school or style. The best critics and the best lay listeners try to do this.

No one, certainly, is expected to like everything. But amid all that creative ferment there is enough variety so that every taste can find something that speaks to it. Sometimes you have to look in out-of-the-way places — in small concert halls, on obscure record labels — to find what you are looking for. It calls for a certain spirit of adventure on the part of the listener — a quality, alas, possessed by all too few of them.

The interested listener can follow the step-by-step procedure alluded to earlier — moving by small increments from the more familiar and traditional-sounding to the more adventurous. It is a means of approaching the new and the different that offers the best hope of making a connection. And when you draw a blank — when you try something far enough out that it simply does not speak to you — you need not feel that you have failed. Musical taste is a sublimely subjective thing. Enjoy what you like and let the rest go.

At the same time, however, remember one other thing: you may want to come back some time to some piece or school of composition that previously seemed incomprehensible and give it another try. The best music has a way of not yielding up all its secrets at a first hearing.

Sometimes it is simply a matter of listener maturation. I would argue that this is true of older music as well. I do not think, for example, that a twelve-year-old is ready for Bach's Saint Matthew Passion or Wagner's Parsifal, two incontestable masterpieces. Beethoven, Brahms and Mozart, no less than Schoenberg and Stockhausen, do not reveal all their depths at a first casual inquiry.

I mentioned earlier the extraordinary variety of styles that today's composers represent. I think the dissemination and understanding of new music has been badly hobbled by this pernicious idea of fashionable "schools." There has been a trendiness, a faddism, an us-against-them cliquishness in the contemporary compositional scene that is decidedly unhealthy. Stories are told of composers who were frozen out of performances or academic posts because they did not conform to the orthodoxy of the moment. Certain periodicals and individual critics become known as advocates for certain schools of composition. There is a lot of unhelpful political jockeying in professional new-music circles.

I doubt that most listeners are much interested in "schools" or fads. They simply want to find a composer or a piece that speaks to them meaningfully and movingly. And they are right to feel that way.

Occasionally the public has cast a decisive veto against some movement promoted from within the establishment. This is a healthy thing, and ought to be encouraged. Real composers write in order to communicate with real audiences; their language may at first seem obscure or complicated, but if the sincerity of purpose is there, the message will eventually get through to the receptive listener. That listener, for his part, has the obligation to be receptive — to go to the concert or approach the recording with open ears and to give the strange new piece his close attention. If it doesn't work for him, fine; but let that not happen because the ears or the mind of the listener were closed, through prejudice or mere laziness.

The listening experience of most serious concertgoers is full of experiences like that — pieces that seemed impenetrable on a first hearing but that opened themselves up more and more at each return visit, eventually entering the inner circle of favorite things. I have had that experience, for example, with the string quartets of Elliott Carter, a composer who makes no pretense to being easily approachable by any casual listener. Carter's approach to composition is up-front analytical and complex. He is not consciously going after classical top-40 status; he is writing what he has to write and trusting to his listeners to stay with him long enough to get his message, complicated though it be. And intimacy thus hard won is oftentimes more lasting and more satisfying than the superficial charm of music that makes an immediate appeal on first hearing.

Having mentioned Carter in that connection, I feel no urge to follow his name with a lengthy list of composers and pieces that might open new ears to "modern music." Everyone will have his own path, his own tastes, his own way of making new musical connections. My suggested listening list will not be yours. The important thing is the succession of gradual incremental steps outlined above, and the willingness to keep ears and mind open to new experiences.

One other thing that I feel has held back the wider public acceptance of new music is what appears to be the curious inability of composers to explain themselves in comprehensible language to a lay audience. Many of them, when asked to furnish program notes or do pre-performance lectures, produce either meaningless moonshine or a morass of technical jargon meant to be understood only by other musicians. Only rarely does one encounter a new piece that is accompanied by a lucid and helpful program note from its creator. This is a pity, but it is a problem that is certainly not confined to our own day, it goes 'way back in musical history.

In that respect, of course, composers are no different from the rest of us; some of them are articulate, some even eloquent, but the vast majority are more or less unable to explain themselves and their work satisfactorily. When the listener is confronted with the largely incomprehensible words of some composer on the occasion of a world premiere, perhaps the best course is simply to ignore them and listen to the music on its own sonic terms. After all, music that does not stand on its own two musical feet but must be supplemented by written explanations is not likely to be a first-class product.

The all-too-infrequent arrival of a composer's commentary on his own work that actually does illuminate it and enhance the listening experience is to be greeted with huzzahs, all the more fervent for being so infrequent.

If only a small percentage of new pieces that come along enter the continuing repertory, no one need be surprised. The same thing has been true in every musical age. The great works of the past that we all know and love are standing, figuratively, on the shoulders of a vast array of lesser works by composers now forgotten. We suffer today rather more than listeners did then from an unfortunate "masterpiece" syndrome that says unless a new score is greeted with immediate acclaim and is somehow anointed a masterwork, it is ipso facto a failure. These are unrealistic expectations to burden a composer with every time he sets pen to score paper. The important thing is that the compositional ferment continues and that new pieces get fair hearings from sympathetic listeners.

It is an exciting process for anyone, layman or professional, to take his part in. Unfortunately, it is also burdened down today with purely economic and even political factors that never arose in past generations. It is harder for a new and ambitious composer to get a fair hearing today than it used to be, and the reasons are mostly irrelevant to art. Being a composer has never been easy, and that is truer today than ever before.

XVIII. BELA BARTOK (1881-1945)

Bela Bartok's highly popular Concerto for Orchestra, one of the very last works he completed before his death, has been described as "modern music for people who hate modern music." This is of course an oversimplification but it carries with it an important kernel of truth. This piece, Bartok's largest orchestral work, unites some very "modern" compositional techniques with lush, almost romantic orchestration and a vein of rich melody that are immediately appealing. And the "marriage" was not accomplished with a shotgun; the two elements exist in happy symbiosis, and the work absolutely deserves its popularity.

In a way this famous piece typifies its composer's place in modern musical history. He was one of a numerous group of composers who served, sometimes perhaps unwittingly, as bridges from the late romantic era into the early 20th century. Some concertgoing malcontent once summed this up in two lines of doggerel:

There's more pleasure per measure in Bach than
Bartok
But Bartok is the rage compared to John Cage

Bartok was a composer of uncompromising honesty
and musical integrity. Like all the best composers he
insisted on going his own way and writing what he had to
write, regardless of the difficulties it created for him or
what the powers of the musical Establishment may have
felt about the matter. He earned a considerable measure
of renown while still alive (though not very much money)
and his stature has continued to grow in the more than
half a century that has passed since he died of leukemia
in a New York City hospital.

One factor that may have slowed his acceptance by
audiences outside his native Hungary was the extraordinary influence exercised over his style by Hungarian
folk music, a type of music not as widely known or
understood outside its country of origin as the folk styles
of countries like France, Italy or England. A very large
portion of Bartok's total output is devoted to arrangements and transcriptions of Balkan-area folk songs.
He spent years traveling about in obscure backwater
regions of the Balkans seeking out old folks who knew
these songs, getting them to sing for him, preserving
the results on primitive recording equipment and then
transcribing the results for publication.

Not surprisingly, this folkish influence is also very
strong in much of his "art music" — major works for

orchestra, chamber music, concert vocal music and the like. It was a part of his personal and musical makeup, along with the expected influences from the world of sophisticated modern art music. This combination, filtered through Bartok's own highly personal musical imagination, gives his concert music as a whole a flavor shared by that of hardly any other major composer in the repertory today. Sometimes in listening to Bartok's music, it is hard to separate out the "art music" strands from the "folkish" influences, so artfully are they intertwined and so subtly do they influence each other as we hear them.

Not many of these Bartok folksong arrangements are heard with any frequency today. If they were, they would cast revealing light on his major pieces for the concert stage.

Besides the striking Concerto for Orchestra, Bartok is most often represented on concert programs today by at least two of his piano concerti, the second violin concerto, the Miraculous Mandarin ballet music, the haunting Music for Strings, Percussion and Celesta and the Divertimento. In smaller forms he is represented by his six astonishing and pathbreaking string quartets, the Contrasts for violin, clarinet and piano, the collection of piano pieces titled Mikrokosmos and the wonderful Sonata for two Pianos and Percussion (which also exists in a version for two pianos and orchestra). His only opera, the one-act Bluebeard's Castle, is infrequently revived, but when it is heard it makes a powerful impression.

One of the traits of Hungarian folk music that profoundly influenced Bartok's art music is its rhythmic irregularity. This is a characteristic found throughout his mature output and one that some people find difficult to get used to. A regular pulse, or what sounds like a regular pulse, will be set going, only to be fractured after a few measures by the insertion or subtraction of extra beats. Accents are sometimes placed on what seem to be "wrong" beats (these tactics are also prominent in Stravinsky's works). Time signatures change often. Yet once the listener comes to terms with this quirky feature, which is to say, once he becomes familiar with it through repeated hearings, the basic attractiveness and expressivity of the music remain.

Bartok also used scale-patterns derived from folk music in his concert-hall pieces, and often sought in his choice of instrumental colorings to evoke the sound and style of folk instruments. All of these characteristics add wonderfully to the richness of his art, even for listeners not familiar with the folk music from which he drew them.

Listeners who may know Bartok's music only through the Concerto for orchestra might want to start enlarging their acquaintance with him by seeking out another piece constructed along rather similar lines – the Music for Strings, Percussion and Celesta. This is a piece in four brilliantly contrasted movements. It bears some fairly obvious stylistic resemblances to the Concerto for Orchestra but for some reason has never achieved a comparable level of popularity.

It opens with a slow and sinuous orchestral fugue marked andante tranquillo based on a highly chromatic theme that moves within a narrow pitch range and is stated at the outset by the violas. The music moves in a kind of glacial, static calm as the various fugal entries complicate the texture and develop into an eerie, densely interwoven web of sound that one imaginative listener once likened to the sound of "wind soughing through trees." There is a long ascent to a moment of climactic tension and then a falling-away as Bartok turns his fugue subject upside-down, as though the music had passed through some sort of Alice in Wonderland looking glass. The final measures are colored by the soft background sound of the celesta. This is a movement constructed of simple basic musical materials yet full of imagination and a kind of eerie, moonlit beauty.

The brilliant and atmospheric use of percussion in this work and in a number of Bartok's other major scores (the second piano concerto and the two-piano sonata come to mind) highlight the composer's interest in elevating that humble orchestral "kitchen" to a stature equal to those of strings, winds and brass in his orchestral palette. Those drums, bells, mallet instruments, cymbals and other such appliances speak in his music with highly expressive voices.

They form, for example, an essential element in one of Bartok's favorite musical styles — music that has been dubbed, for better or worse, "night music."

Such episodes, in which the sounds of insects and birds and the general air of mystery associated with the idea of night are featured, occur in many of Bartok's most important scores, and in both his orchestral and chamber music.

The third movement of the Music for Strings, Percussion and Celesta is a prime example of the genre. It begins with a mysterious tapped-out rhythmic pattern on the solo xylophone (marked with Bartok's characteristic care as to dynamic level, expression and rhythmic freedom), answered by mysterious glissando rumblings on the timpani. Strings join in with mysterious chromatic musings. Cellos briefly propose the fugue theme from the first movement, but they are answered only by eerie trills in the high strings and weird staccato interjections by the piano. The movement progresses as additional instruments become involved, but there is very little of traditional rhythm or melody to be heard. All is ghostly atmosphere, uncannily involving and weirdly beautiful. This remarkable movement (only about six and a half minutes long) ends much as it began with the same high-pitched coded message from the xylophone and soft taps on the timpani. This is not music for the concertgoer whose tastes run only as far forward as Strauss and Mahler, but it is eloquent and beautiful music nonetheless.

Bartok's interest in percussion effects extended to his piano writing, which very often treats the piano as a member of that family rather than as a lyrical instrument.

Pianists and recitalgoers may know his famous Allegro Barbaro as one example, and the second of his three piano concertos in particular is another.

There is no medium, however, in which Bartok's influence was greater than in that of the string quartet, a notoriously difficult genre for even master composers to deal with.

He wrote six quartets. They cover a period of about 30 years in his creative life and they are generally regarded as the most important and influential body of work by a 20th century master in the quartet medium (Shostakovich and possibly Elliott Carter are his only serious rivals in that regard).

It is regrettable that chamber music, by its very nature, does not get the same mass exposure that orchestral music does. The string quartets of Beethoven and Mozart, to take two obvious examples, bulk as large and as significantly in those composers' outputs as do their symphonies, but consider the degree of public familiarity of quartets versus symphonies in each case! Bartok, who wrote no symphonies as such (except for juvenilia), made a major statement in the quartet medium; it is so recognized by critics and musicologists, but certainly not by the listening public at large, which knows mainly his orchestral music.

These six quartets sum up Bartok's art as a composer. There is an almost Mahlerian emotional intensity about the first quartet (written in 1908-1909), yet the fingerprints of Bartok's mature style are already hearable in it. The second quartet (1915-1917) is one of those fascinating works that seems to sit astride the stylistic fault line dividing the "romantic" era from the "modern" (as I have mentioned, Schoenberg's splendid second quartet inhabits that same musical landscape.) The third quartet (1927) is the shortest and most enigmatic of the six.

The fourth and fifth (respectively 1928 and 1934) show Bartok in his full stylistic maturity, with their characteristic mixture of dissonant modern textures with outbursts of peasant folk dance and intense inward-looking drama. They also both illustrate another characteristic of his style by their employment of a five-movement "arch" form, in which the third movement is a musical and emotional focal point around which two pairs of related movements swing — the second and fourth and also the first and fifth.

The sixth quartet, dating from 1939, is unique in employing a slow, meditative theme as introduction to each of its four movements. The theme (marked mesto — sad) is differently dressed for each appearance, but is instantly recognizable. In the second movement it introduces a vigorous, though somewhat tipsy, march rhythm, and in the third a vigorous dance-like episode which Bartok labeled burletta. In the quartet's eloquent final movement the mesto theme becomes the main business of a slow, meditative piece, somber in tone but sometimes sounding almost sweet in its air of resignation. The calm, reflective piece ultimately dies away peacefully

— in a clear major tonality.

These quartets are not perhaps "easy listening" for traditional ears, but they are intensely dramatic and emotionally truthful pieces by a man who had important things to say in sound and who was not about to compromise in his musical language.

Bartok was not (like Puccini, for instance) a composer content to work in an already formulated musical language; nor was he a composer (like Schoenberg) who consciously set out to create a whole new musical language for himself. He simply followed his own star wherever it led him and did not seem to care what the solemn keepers of musicological pigeonholes would make of him.

He came from a country that had produced its share of international musical figures, yet most of them (Liszt, for example) had elected to make their careers on the wider musical stage afforded by places like Vienna (which, after all, is only about 140 miles from Budapest). There is certainly a strong Hungarian flavor to much of Liszt's music, but it is very often decked out and dressed up in the flashy garb of mainstream Central European virtuoso music making. Bartok (and his compatriot Zoltan Kodaly) elected to remain truer to their Hungarian musical roots. They thereby forfeited the mass audience appeal that Liszt had attracted in his day; but Bartok in particular managed to carve for himself his own central place in the mid-20th century repertory.

It was not an easy triumph for Bartok. A man who heard him perform his second piano concerto with the Cleveland Orchestra during a concert tour of America in the early 1940s once told me a touching story about him. The Cleveland audience, my informant said, had not much liked the vigorous, percussive piece. Applause was little more than polite. But my friend had been touched by the music and went backstage to introduce himself to the pianist-composer. His action was motivated in part, he admitted, because he felt sorry for Bartok.

Bartok was evidently glad to find at least one appreciative listener. They fell to talking and Bartok ended by innocently telling his new friend that, being in America, he would like to go somewhere where he might hear "the boogies-woogies." They made a date for the next night after the concert, but Bartok was careful to warn his American friend: "You will have to pay. I have no money. I send everything I earn back home to my family."

And thus it was the next night that Bartok and his friend ended up at a jazz joint where the great composer listened to the work of the noted blind jazz pianist Art Tatum. Fascinated, he expressed an interest in meeting Tatum and questioning him about the musical means he used to create some of his jazz effects.

The meeting proved awkward. Tatum had no clear idea who Bartok was and he was puzzled by the composer's academic inquiries. Their meeting ended with Tatum delivering what amounted to his own version of the famous Louis Armstrong saying: "If you have to ask what it is, you'll never know!"

This incident happened just before Bartok fled Europe in the face of the rising Nazi threat to his homeland, and came to the United States, where he lived the last five years of his life. The story of these five years, in which Bartok enjoyed only intermittent periods of employment and financial security despite the efforts of influential friends who knew his worth, has been told many times. Mixed in with the financial story, of course, is the story of the composer's declining health. He spent one summer in Vermont, another in North Carolina, and additional time in upstate New York in search of good health. It is said that the commission for the Concerto for Orchestra, proffered by Serge Koussevitzky, was actually a factor in prolonging Bartok's life; the stimulation of working on this superb score revitalized his energy in some mysterious but well-attested way.

At the very end of his life he was working furiously to finish his third piano concerto and to create a viola concerto requested by William Primrose. The piano concerto, still one of his most popular and frequently-heard works, was complete except for the scoring of the last 17 measures; his son had ruled the bar-lines for those measures on score paper for him, and Bartok had written the Hungarian word vege (the end) at the conclusion; but he never made it. Those bars were completed by his colleague Tibor Serly.

There has been a lot of posthumous debate over

whether America mistreated and ignored this great composer living in its midst. It is the kind of argument with which Americans often like to lacerate themselves post facto. There is probably no definitive answer at this late date; but Bela Bartok has taken his place, albeit tardily, among the ranks of the century's true masters.

Interlude V: What Makes the Critic Run?

The exact nature of the music critic's job seems to mystify just about everyone in the music world except the critic himself. Performers and composers love to denounce the critic, audiences often ignore him, a fair number of people think he is simply unnecessary, concert managers and promoters sometimes act as if his every word were Holy Writ — and just about everyone thinks in his heart of hearts that he could do the job better than the critic can.

I speak with some authority about this arcane craft, having served as chief music critic on a large metropolitan daily newspaper for 28 years. From this admittedly biased standpoint, I would argue that the critic's function is a necessary one, and that when done well it makes a valuable contribution to musical life.

At the same time, I think it is possible to grant the critic too much power. In music, as in politics, that is a dangerous business.

People who are just beginning to take a serious

interest in classical music often tend to overrate the critic's importance. They automatically assume that he is some learned savant whose word must carry great weight. There seems to be something about the printed word in a newspaper, magazine or book that lends the writer an undeserved aura of authority.

Let's start with something that seems painfully obvious: the critic is a human being just like the rest of us. He may have a good deal of specialized training in music, but he is still no superman whose every word must be regarded as Gospel. A respected American critic once summed up his creed in these words: "Criticism — hell, what is it but your own opinion?"

That word "opinion" is important. Music criticism is a slippery, subjective business that deals in intangible values and unquantifiable personal reactions to music. You are free to disagree with your local critic, and he is not necessarily free to sneer that he is "right" and you are "wrong" — unless of course some item of verifiable fact is involved. I would encourage the newcomer to classical music to give the critic a kind of probationary period during which his likes and dislikes are noted, his personal prejudices catalogued and allowed for. Then, when you have the measure of the man (or woman), you can read him with that in mind and decide for yourself whether you agree or disagree. This can be a very stimulating and enjoyable exercise.

The best critics, I feel, try to be guides and teachers rather than law givers. They try to enlighten their audience, not to issue commands to it. They can also serve the very valuable purpose of helping to raise the level of musical sophistication and awareness in their local community. They can point out worthwhile things that are going on that might otherwise get lost in the blare of media hype too often devoted to more "newsworthy" but less substantive events.

The best critics, too, have quirky personal biases that they make no attempt to hide. They break lances for obscure or unpopular causes. They shine their spotlight on worthy but little-known corners of concert life, and they also demand to know why certain events or performers of great importance are more or less ignored.

A perceptive critic can open up the listener's ears and mind to things he may have missed while listening even to familiar pieces. He can point out musical relationships, compositional procedures that may even pass unnoticed because they are so obvious, like the famous letter in the Poe short story.

The great composer-critic Virgil Thomson once defined, in his inimitable way, the qualifications of the music critic. Very simple, said Thomson, you have to know everything there is to know about music, and you have to know how to write.

The first of those points is obviously impossible. The second is a gift that some have and some do not; but it is just as important as the knowledge of music. You can be the most learned musical scholar in the universe, but if you are unable to express yourself in writing that seizes and maintains the attention of your readers, you will not succeed as a critic. You have to know your field, but you must never be dull. (Unfortunately, even poor music critics can often write well.)

In my experience there are two main types of music critics: musicians who can write (or who think they can), and writers who know music (or who think they do). Very fine critics have come from both camps, and so indeed have some perfectly dreadful ones. There is a distinguished roster of great composers, from Robert Schumann to Virgil Thomson, who worked as critics. The list would include Berlioz, Debussy and Hugo Wolf among others. Berlioz was arguably the finest writer of prose among all composers (read his wonderful memoirs for confirmation of this).

We pass over in silence the fact that Schumann and Wolf both ended their days as inmates of insane asylums.

Most of these composer-critics were not happy in their critical jobs. Often they did it because they needed the money. And all of them are remembered today mainly for the great music they wrote, not really for their critical labors.

Composers often do not make the most readable critics because they lack the common touch. They become so involved in the technical minutiae of the work under review that their prose can be understood only by another highly trained composer. I have served for some years as program-note editor for an orchestra that specializes in new music by living composers, and I can testify that the notes many of them submit about their own works are simply unreadable. In one or two cases there were items in their notes about their own music that were simply incorrect.

Among critics who were primarily writers rather than musicians, the most famous example is George Bernard Shaw, who functioned as a critic on two London papers before beginning his career as playwright and general societal gadfly. His music criticism makes lively reading even today. There is in fact a long tradition in England of laymen who turned themselves into fine music critics by sheer personal headwork and persistence and without terribly much formal musical training. One of the finest of the lot, the great Wagner authority Ernest Newman, was actually a music-loving bank clerk named William Roberts until he decided to turn himself into a new man in earnest.

It is often the fate of the poor critic, even a good one, to be remembered by his mistakes. The great Viennese critic Edward Hanslick is remembered today almost exclusively because of his fierce opposition to Wagner. But if you read a collection of Hanslick's writings, you will find him an insightful and fair-minded fellow who wrote extremely well. Then there was the case of the Englishman Henry F. Chorley, who had a blind spot for the operas of Verdi and has been dismissed as a tin ear for that reason. But Chorley was a lively and intelligent writer, as a reading of some of his collected criticism will show.

It would be foolish to pretend that there are no unqualified people acting as music critics these days. Of course there are, especially on smaller newspapers around the U.S. Horror stories are gleefully repeated by performers and composers who feel themselves abused. But efforts are under way, largely sponsored by the Music Critics Association of North America (MCANA) to correct the situation by raising the educational level of younger critics through a program of workshops and seminars. I have been involved in running this program over the years, and there have been several notable success stories resulting from it.

The problem currently is that the whole field of music criticism is shrinking as the number of newspapers declines and those that remain devote less and less space to serious arts criticism and more and more to pop culture or trendy "profile" pieces. The "new media" — television, the Internet — have not as yet gotten into music criticism in any really effective way. It is a craft that seems uniquely wedded to the printed word, rather than the spoken or cyber-transmitted word.

One charge commonly leveled at the critical fraternity is that these people are "parasites." In general they do not perform themselves, or compose music. They simply sit in their aisle seat, pencils poised, and work their malevolent will, or so the folklore goes.

I would argue that this is precisely correct (except

for that bit about malevolence), and also it is precisely why the critic is such a valuable fellow. He has no vested interest, no ax to grind, no scores to settle (most of the time). He is akin to the umpire at the ballpark or the referee at the tennis match. He tries his best to "call them as he sees them." You can argue that he may miss a call now and then, as umpires and referees also do, but it seems to me self-evident that some such person is a necessary part of our musical life. He should be well trained, honest and a good writer. If he is not, someone else should get the job, someone who meets those requirements.

During my years as an active critic, many a person thought to pay me a compliment by saying "I read you constantly, and I always agree with you." This bothered me a good deal. I was sometimes tempted to reply, perhaps ungraciously, "That's too bad. Why aren't you thinking for yourself?"

I thought of my job as stimulating people to draw their own conclusions about what we had heard together in some concert hall. Agreement or disagreement was not really the point; the important thing was to go back over the musical experience we had in common and think about it more deeply — in a word, to take it more seriously, to realize that music is important to one's life.

I used to draw a homely analogy to show what I thought the experience of hearing music was all about. Three people are involved — composer, performer and listener. If any one of them is not present, obviously no communication is taking place. The critic I pictured as a kind of intellectual maintenance technician whose job was to keep the electric current flowing in all directions along that three-way circuit. Certainly from composer to performer to listener — but also from performer to composer, from listener to performer, and so on. There must be free interplay among all three poles and in all the possible different directions — and the critic is the person who can make that happen.

The popular image of the critic as an ill-tempered ogre who is out to find fault with whatever he hears is a gross libel on the critical craft. Most critics, believe it or not, are people who genuinely love music and care deeply about its future. They want to have great experiences in the concert hall or the opera house. They do not enjoy writing negative reviews. But they also labor under an obligation simply to tell the truth. It is possible to tell the truth without being nasty about it; you do not, as the saying goes, have to call a spade a shovel. You need the verbal facility to say what has to be said plainly and honestly, and without malice. It is not the easiest job in the world, especially when it must be done in a terrible hurry immediately after a concert and with the Demon Deadline staring you in the face. Words are tricky objects, not easily lined up in perfect order on demand. But it can be done.

The music critic, however, faces a special problem here. Music is the most ephemeral of all the arts, the one least amenable to expression in words. It is transient and invisible and it deals mainly in abstract sounds, not in visual images or concrete words. There are really no words to describe music; if there were, you might say there would be no need for the music. So the critic must borrow terminology from the other arts, or from wherever he finds it handy. This is the source of much of the moonshine-tinged jargon that infects music criticism and makes it sound like bad abstract poetry. The critic is in essence trying to describe the indescribable. It can't be done, perhaps, but all the honor lies in the attempt.

Those in the music business — the composers, performers, concert presenters, and press agents — tend to look upon the critic as a kind of necessary evil. He can be a source of publicity — "good ink" is the trade expression. They want quotes that will look good on resumes and in publicity brochures. This should properly be none of the critic's concern. He has to write what he feels is true, and never mind the consequences.

Critics, especially those on daily newspapers, have to also resist the great American urge to be specialists. They cannot concentrate on one or two areas of special musical interest and "wing it" for everything else. They have to have a fairly detailed acquaintance with all sorts of repertory — not just operas and the symphonic repertory, but early music, chamber music, piano music, lieder repertory, organ music, church music, electronic music, the latest trends in contemporary concert music, and a whole host of other fields that come up routinely in their day-by-day rounds. No one, *pace* Virgil Thomson, can know everything. We all have strong suits and weak suits. The work of the critic is a constant course of musical self-education. New things are coming along all the time and he must keep up with them. I am the first to admit that I learned more after becoming a full-time critic than I knew before I took the job. It is no job for the complacently self-satisfied.

I have no idea where music criticism is headed. If the Internet ever begins to realize its potential in this field, it could completely change the modus operandi of the music critic and introduce him to a whole new audience. There are stirrings in that direction even now, but no one knows where they will lead. There is grave doubt these days even about the future of the printed daily newspaper, so it may be that the critic of the future will inhabit some other medium, probably in cyberspace.

But until that happens, the critic must continue to strive to make himself useful and valuable in the musical community as guide, tastemaker, teacher, and explorer of the unknown. He should not worry about being the feared arbiter of the worthy and the unworthy. That is a popular prejudice that should really be laid to rest forever. The music critic has a very important role to play in musical life, but it has already become quite different from the role he was assigned when the whole idea of criticism was new, and further unimaginable changes may be just over the horizon.

XIX. AARON COPLAND (1900-1990)

The noted composer and critic Virgil Thomson once referred to Aaron Copland as "the natural president of American music." It was a felicitous phrase. Copland not only became celebrated through the communicative power of his music, he was also an influential organizer, promoter, polemicist, teacher and general all-around factotum in the service of one of the world's most fragile endangered species — the American composer of "serious" music.

Our celebrity-oriented culture tends to make pop celebrities out of performers rather than composers. They are the ones who get the feature profiles in newspapers and who get shown on television. But the truly important figure in our musical life, or in any country's musical life, has to be the composer, the man who actually creates the product.

In America today the serious composer gets little recognition or honor, unless he happens to be a media celebrity like Leonard Bernstein. But the Bernsteins on the American scene are the exceptions. Aaron Copland chose the life of the composer for himself, stuck with it doggedly and successfully for almost 70 years, and devoted a good deal of his surplus time and energy to trying to bring some overdue recognition to his fellow composers. It was an uphill struggle but an honorable one. Whether it was actually a more important activity than his composing is something that only time will tell. Offhand, I doubt it.

It was surely remarkable that Copland actually became a kind of second-string media celebrity himself — not, certainly in Bernstein's league, but at least a man whose name and accomplishments were recognized by many people outside the world of "serious" music. He was even considered a big enough "fish" to be dragged before a congressional committee during the days of anti-Communist hysteria in the 1950s – a kind of backhanded recognition of his status in our cultural life. Copland survived the encounter unscathed; he discusses it frankly in the oral history memoirs he prepared with Vivian Perlis in the last decade of his life.

Copland always said that his aim was to write music that would be instantly recognizable as "American" in sound. He spoke of the listener who tunes in on the radio in mid-piece and, while perhaps unable to name the precise work being performed, he can tell by its characteristic sound whether it is French, Russian or Italian. Copland wanted to establish a similar identity for American music, and in a way he was uniquely qualified for the job, being himself a very "American" product.

There are, of course, many different kinds of "Americans," most of them with roots overseas. Copland's immediate ancestors were Lithuanian and Russian Jews who had emigrated to this country and traveled widely around it (Illinois, Texas, ultimately New York) in search of a livelihood. This is one of the classic "American" stories and somehow one gets the feeling that it left a distinct imprint on the music of the man who came to be described as the "composer from Brooklyn." Even his appearance — tall, rangy, gangling, with a big hawk nose and a thick Lower East Side New York accent — was one of our classic "American" looks, and not at all that of your stereotypical "serious" composer. I once wrote that Copland looked like a friendly neighborhood butcher, and I see no reason to alter that description.

Copland was one of the earliest of that swarm of Americans who flocked to France early in this century to come under the spell of the great teacher Nadia Boulanger. But he never really succumbed to the French musical aesthetic. His style changed fairly drastically during his long career, but no one ever doubted that he was always his own man.

It is perhaps too soon after his death to attempt any long-term judgment on his eventual place in American music, but it seems obvious that he will bulk very large indeed. He was a take-charge person in an era when American musical expression emerged from its European cocoon and began to speak energetically for itself. Also, he was definitely in the mainstream of musical activity where he could make a palpable difference, not — like Charles Ives — off on the sidelines composing epoch-making works that few if any people even knew about until years later.

Many commentators have remarked that Copland had two distinct styles — the folksy, overtly "American" and quasi-popular style of works like Appalachian Spring and Billy the Kid, and an abstract academic style that produced a string of works that are less known and less often performed but are nonetheless important. Prominent among these are three major pieces for piano solo — the Piano Variations, Piano Fantasy and Piano Sonata. Add to this mix the fact that Copland made significant contributions to music for the movies and had a lively interest in jazz, and you begin to sense what a wide-ranging, well-rounded and ultimately influential fellow he was.

Copland is the only composer featured in these essays that I have met personally, so a few remarks gleaned from perhaps seven or eight meetings over the years may not be out of place. I saw him and spoke with him in a number of different settings, public and private, and I was always struck by the man's utter naturalness, his total lack of "airs" or of the vanity that we tend to associate with artistic accomplishment. He was equally at ease, whether in the company of callow college undergraduates or of the musically high-and-mighty.

Once, during the heyday of the electronic-music

fad, a college student asked him whether he was at all interested in that means of composition. Of course, as a professional musician he was "interested," Copland replied with utter candor, but it was nothing he felt he had any aptitude for, and so he left it to others who did.

"I'm the kind of person," he summed up, "who when he walks into a room and flips the light switch and the light goes on — I'm happy!" I cannot imagine very many other composers answering that question in those terms.

I also chatted with him just as he was approaching his 65th birthday and remarked jokingly that I hoped he had no plans to retire.

"I can't retire," the celebrated composer said with a chuckle, "I've never held a regular job. I have nothing to retire from!"

Some years later we were on a panel discussion together and Copland was talking about his late-in-life career as a conductor. He started conducting mainly to be able to give definitive performances of his own music, he said, and found that he enjoyed the experience. Besides, he had been composing for so long that he felt he had earned the right to do something else. To the suggestion that he should not give up composing considering the great wealth of music he had left us, his self-deprecatory answer was "Oh, give me a break, will you? I've been composing for 50 years — don't you think its time I did something else?"

Copland's strategy for achieving a recognizable "American" sound in his music involved, of course, the use of folk tunes and American subjects. There are well-known examples of this in works like the ballet Billy The Kid, the Lincoln Portrait, the Pulitzer Prize-winning Appalachian Spring, and of course in the two sets of Old American Songs, which are his own transcriptions of folk material.

But he also tried to sound "American" by the quality of his orchestration, with its characteristic widely spaced chordal intervals and its rhythmic verve. This is a less tangible way of attacking the problem, to be sure, but the resulting sound is, first of all, quite uniquely and recognizably his, and secondly it somehow suggests the American spirit and the American landscape.

Copland was also interested in jazz as an American contribution to world music, and this interest is reflected in several of his better-known works, notably the Piano Concerto and the Clarinet Concerto. But Copland was the first to admit that the "jazz-influenced" sections of those works were not "real jazz." They were jazz as filtered through the mind and imagination of a thoroughly classically trained composer, and one writing for the concert hall rather than the night club or the dance hall.

The stylistic cleavage between Copland's "American-style" works and his more abstract pieces is quite distinct in purely technical terms, yet when you listen to them side by side the characteristic Copland sound and technique of orchestration betray the fact that they were both written by the same man. The technical procedures may be vastly different, but the aural fingerprints are there.

Perhaps the clearest way to demonstrate the two musical sides of Copland's personality might be to listen seriatim to two of his vocal works, the famous sets of Old American Songs and the cycle of Emily Dickinson Songs. The Old American Songs are a commonplace of our musical life these days. They are skillfully done, to be sure, but they are merely Copland's glosses on already existing folk tunes and as such do not represent him in any really meaningful way. The Dickinson Songs — hardly ever performed nowadays — are no less expressive and, in their different way, beautiful, but they are couched in Copland's more abstract style and have no truck with folksiness for its own sake. If some of our great recital singers were a little more adventurous in planning their programs, these songs might achieve the acceptance they deserve. Another lesser-known Copland piece that deserve wider circulation is his lovely Nonet for strings.

Copland has been fortunate in that at least one of his large-scale works, the Appalachian Spring ballet suite, is also one of his best-known and widely performed works. The piece sums up his style in its rhythmic exuberance, its typically Coplandesque orchestral coloring and its imaginative use of a folk tune, the now-famous Simple Gifts which takes center stage near the end of the piece.

For years audiences knew this fine suite only through the full-orchestra version that Copland prepared after he had completed the original ballet. Only recently are we beginning to get more and more performances of the original version for 13 instruments. I love both versions and cannot really recommend one over the other. The only problem a listener has, it seems to me, is getting the sound of the familiar big-orchestra version out of his ears so he can listen to the chamber version on its own terms.

Among Copland's other "greatest hits" is the Lincoln Portrait, a piece often dismissed these days as a piece of simplistic wartime propaganda. I would like unfashionably to insist that it is rather more than that. I find it a very stirring and impressive piece, imaginatively put together, dramatically effective and quite beautiful. (I should confess that I have a twofold special interest here: I am an American history buff with a great interest in Abraham Lincoln, and I once performed the Lincoln Portrait narration under the baton of Copland himself; if that disqualifies me on grounds of personal bias, so be it.)

Copland's only opera for an adult audience (discounting The Second Hurricane, which was written for performance by high schoolers) is The Tender Land, a folksy piece in his "Americana" style that in some aspects of its plot prefigures William Inge's famous play Picnic. It is a very worthwhile piece that ought to be better known.

I have already mentioned, among Copland's more abstract pieces, his three major works for piano solo. The Piano Variations also exists in an orchestral version, which, if anything, reinforces its steely percussiveness. Being short — about 12 minutes — the piece also achieves a fair number of performances in both piano and orchestral guise. It seems to me that the true "orphan" among these three works is the large-scale Piano Fantasy, a work of great imagination and impressive emotional power that more pianists should dare to present to the public.

This dichotomy between Copland's two styles may turn out to be a real obstacle to any eventual determination of his place in America's musical history. There are those, mainly in academia, who will say that Copland was only a "serious" composer in his abstract pieces, and that his large (and far more popular) body of "Americana" works represents a lowering of standards that compromises his place in the musical firmament. Then there are those (mainly in the general concertgoing public) who admire and enjoy the "American" works but cannot be bothered to deal with the more abstract pieces, regarding them as pretentious and somehow a betrayal of the composer's "real" self. It is sad but true that this sort of reasoning plays an important part in arriving at any final qualitative estimate of a composer like Aaron Copland. It is a kind of game played by musical cognoscenti that only clouds the issue of the worth of the music itself.

No one seems to have realized that Copland may

have been equally sincere in working in both styles, that both of them are equally "Coplandesque" and that each should be judged, not against the other, but against whatever absolute standards of good and bad the individual listener brings to the experience. Copland deals with this whole issue, by the way, in a very candid way in the two previously mentioned volumes of oral history that he produced with Yale musicologist Vivian Perlis (St. Martin's Press, 1984 and 1989).

Aaron Copland's long and varied career forms an essential bridge from the backward-looking musical culture of 1920s America (when Edward MacDowell was generally nominated as the best composer we had yet produced) to the busy and fragmented scene that followed World War 2. He chose not to plunge into the avant-garde musical culture that set in about 1960 (though he did flirt with twelve-tone procedures in a few of his later works,) but by that time he was established as a kind of father figure whose position was unassailable even by those who began to consider him old-fashioned.

As his composing activity slacked off after 1950 or so he took on the aura of a kind of living musical monument, touring college campuses and serving as mentor to the American musical world in general. He could look back with a smile to the 1920s when he himself was considered a wild young radical intent on disturbing the slumbers of symphony audiences with works like his Symphony for Organ and Orchestra, a piece championed by Serge

Koussevitzky in Boston and roundly denounced by old-line Boston Symphony patrons when Koussevitzky inflicted in on them.

As these words are written, Aaron Copland has been dead for a decade. His music is still heard frequently in this country, though perhaps not so frequently as during his lifetime. The question is a haunting one — how much of it will we be hearing thirty, forty, fifty years from now? Will he be fated, as many have been before him, to be represented only by less important and shorter pieces like El Salon Mexico and the ubiquitous Fanfare for the Common Man? Or will he be honored as pioneer teacher and polemicist while being more or less forgotten as composer?

Who knows? I would only suggest that a nation which has produced superb major pieces like Appalachian Spring and the Piano Fantasy would be foolish to forget them.

XX. DMITRI SHOSTAKOVICH (1906-1975)

It is well nigh impossible to consider the music of Dmitri Shostakovich without reference to his sad and tumultuous life story. Much of the notoriety he achieved during his lifetime had more to do with political than with musical matters. Even today, almost a generation after his death, the two remain inextricably entwined, and the whole truth of the matter is still by no means certain.

Shostakovich was a boy wonder. His cheeky first symphony, written while he was still a conservatory student, put him on the musical map of his native Russia to stay and raised hopes for a bright future – hopes that were amply fulfilled. That youthful symphony is still part of the worldwide standard symphonic repertory today, and rightly so.

Shostakovich had the misfortune to grow up under the Stalin dictatorship in Russia, and to fall victim to its heavy-handed regimentation of the arts as tools of the Soviet State. He was denounced and disciplined for his musical "errors," and he made the ritual confessions and apologies that were so prominent a part of that sorry chapter in Russian history. The Soviets even paraded him outside their borders once or twice for political propaganda purposes. By all accounts he was consumed in the last years of his life by a corrosive cynicism and bitterness that came close to drying up his creative impulses. It may well be the saddest personal story in the whole long history of music.

During all those years, however, he somehow kept producing music. Only now, more than 20 years after his death and some years after the political conditions that dogged his days have disappeared, are we beginning the job of taking stock and finally determining his true place in musical history. So far at least, the verdict appears to be favorable; he stands higher in both critical and popular favor now than he has at any time since the days of U.S.-Soviet wartime collaboration. This is an outcome that very few would have predicted twenty years ago.

It might be useful at this point to give a brief survey of the ups and downs of his reputation over the years. As a young composer (starting with the days of that remarkable first symphony, premiered in 1924 when he was all of 18) he was known as a cheeky, irreverent fellow, enormously talented but somewhat erratic. His reputation grew steadily and spread to the west through such works as the Age of Gold ballet with its famous polka, and the famous opera Lady Macbeth of Mzensk, which was the occasion for the first of his several clashes with the Soviet government's ideological police force.

The notable works kept coming — the set of piano preludes in 1932, the delightful first piano concerto the next year, the world-famous (and still popular) fifth symphony in 1937.

Then with the outbreak of World War 2 and the heady era of U.S.-Soviet wartime friendship, he became something more than a mere composer — he became a kind of folk-hero, a human symbol of the heroic Russian resistance to the Nazis. This all came to a head with the premiere of his ambitious seventh symphony in 1941 and its subsequent arrival in the west. The story of how Shostakovich began this sprawling work while working as an air raid warden in besieged Leningrad and of how the score was spirited out to the west by a circuitous route, became front-page news. The American premiere (conducted by Toscanini, a conductor not at all noted for his sympathy for contemporary music) received enormous publicity, and made Shostakovich a full-fledged popular hero.

Then of course came the end of the war, the onset of the "Cold War" and the rapid souring of U.S.-Soviet relations. Shostakovich's stock tumbled precipitously. Critics suddenly began dismissing him as a trifler and a vulgarian. Performances of his music in the west dried up to a trickle. Only the first and fifth symphonies kept a secure place in the standard symphonic repertory.

By the time of his death in 1975 (after a long period of declining health), Shostakovich's reputation in the West was in tatters. It took a long period of reassessment after that for it to begin a slow upward climb. This new ascent was helped along by two events that happened in quick succession at the end of the 1980's — the publication of a book that purported to be his suppressed biography, and the collapse of the Soviet Union.

The book was Testimony, put together by a young Russian musician named Solomon Volkov from what he insisted were long hours of conversation with Shostakovich, and allegedly authenticated by the composer himself before his death. It painted a truly grim picture of Shostakovich as a deeply bitter man, ground down by bureaucratic enemies who made him miserable and forced him to maintain a public persona that denied his real self. It put up for discussion radical reassessments and reinterpretations of many of Shostakovich's best-known works, including the famous fifth and seventh symphonies.

Testimony was a literary and musical bombshell. The Soviet regime denounced it as a fraud and insisted Volkov was an unprincipled adventurer who had sold the composer out for money. Musicians who had known Shostakovich lined up pro and con.

The authenticity of this book has never been proven beyond doubt, but the dust has settled somewhat over the years. The general consensus among those who knew Shostakovich best (including cellist-conductor Mstislav Rostropovich and the composer's son Maxim) is that the general outlines of Volkov's bitter portrait are true, but that many specific details in the book were elaborated or exaggerated by Volkov in order to make himself appear more intimate with the composer than he actually was. I believe it was Maxim Shostakovich who summed up Testimony as an accurate book about his father, but in many details not strictly accurate.

The collapse of the Soviet regime (which coincidentally followed quickly after the publication of Testimony) created the conditions for a dispassionate and non-political assessment of Shostakovich's work. His reputation has been steadily on the rise as this process has gone ahead. For years he was routinely bracketed with his contemporary Sergei Prokofieff in the history of modern Russian music, and for most of that time Prokofieff (who had his own serious troubles with the Soviet cultural commissars) was regarded as the greater of the two composers. At present, however, Shostakovich appears to have been reinstalled in the top spot. Such judgments are, of course, highly subjective and more than a little silly in artistic terms, but they are the daily stuff of musical controversy.

Shostakovich was never an avant-gardist as the term is understood in the west. This was partly due to the "socialist realism" concept promoted by the Soviet state under which he had to operate, but also due to his own musical instincts. There is a populist vein in even his most serious work, an obvious consciousness that there is an audience out there waiting and wanting to connect with the composer's message. Many critics have found fault with this, seeing in the coexistence of cheekiness and seriousness in his output (oftentimes within a single work) a failure of compositional taste. Their predecessors said the same thing, of course, about Mahler, a composer Shostakovich greatly admired and to whom he is often compared.

Shostakovich was unusual among modern composers in keeping up a lifelong interest in the formal symphony; he wrote 15 of them and they form a kind of musical autobiography stretching from his student days to the year before his death. It was said that he had completed two movements of a 16th symphony before he died, but these have not come to light.

Four or five of those 15 symphonies are heard with fair frequency these days, but only the fifth has maintained its worldwide popularity consistently since the day of its premiere. It is a work of extraordinary brilliance and gusto, tuneful and dramatic and well deserving of its popularity. Its central feature is the famous slow movement (largo), a long, serene meditation that never slips over into boredom despite its lack of superficial "excitement." There are similar meditative movements in a number of Shostakovich's other works; he has been dubbed in some quarters as a supreme master of the "largo."

With the once-famous seventh symphony again being performed and recorded fairly often after long years in the symphonic wilderness, one can at least now try to listen to it objectively and judge it one purely musical grounds. The extensive opening movement, with its famous march theme that works up from a whisper to a thundering full-orchestra fortissimo still seems to me to work supremely well, despite the scorn that has been heaped upon it by a generation of critics. In general I would say the seventh is a bit too long and repetitive for its content, but that does not mean it has nothing to say to us in purely musical terms.

The delightful small-scale ninth symphony also seems to hold its own now that the political and social conditions surrounding its birth (the immediate postwar period) have vanished; this is a piece eminently deserving of more exposure than it gets.

Among the later symphonies, perhaps the most noteworthy is the extraordinary 14th symphony, for two vocal soloists and chamber orchestra. It is a setting of a series of poems about death. A committed performance of this work can be a moving, even shattering experience despite the work's overall serious tone bordering on morbidity.

Shostakovich also made a major impact on the string quartet with his series of 16 works in that form. The eighth is the best known; it was even turned into a small-scale "symphony" in an arrangement for string orchestra by Rudolf Barshai. But there are a number of others in the series that ought to be better known.

Both of Shostakovich's piano concertos are on the fringe of the standard repertory today, as is the first of his cello concertos and his second violin concerto. Pianists occasionally look into his sharp-edged little piano preludes. His once notorious opera Lady Macbeth of Mzensk is being performed more often, and his bouncy Festival Overture has made it into the pops-concert repertory. Shostakovich exemplifies what Benjamin Britten was also demonstrating at just about the same time — that it is possible to write basically tonal, more-or-less traditionally-oriented music, even toward the end of the 20th century, that speaks both profoundly and originally to an audience of willing ears.

This seems to me important. It is indeed possible to be "original" without being in the vanguard of experimental technique. A composer need not seek to do every time out something that has never been done before, in a manic pursuit of "originality." It is possible to adopt existing techniques but simply to fill them with sounds of such obvious conviction that an audience is reached, even moved.

Shostakovich has been criticized for what some see as a "vulgar" streak in his stylistic makeup. There are episodes even in some of his large-scale, seriously intended works that some see as unworthy of a "serious" composer. The famous march episode in the opening movement of the seventh symphony, referred to above, is one such episode; it is generally agreed that Bela Bartok, for one, was so appalled at the "banality" of Shostakovich's march tune that he poked fun at it — complete with obvious orchestral "razzberries" — in the intermezzo interrotto movement of his great Concerto for Orchestra (1945).

The same charge, as previously noted, was routinely levied against Mahler (and still is, in some quarters). It may be that a few more years and a good many more performances of some of these pieces have to accumulate before we can come to terms with this aspect of Shostakovich's musical personality.

I personally think this will happen, and that the charge of "banality" will not stick over the long haul. One tiny piece of evidence on that score concerns the last of Shostakovich's symphonies, No. 15, completed just shortly before his death and generally greeted coldly by the gatekeepers of musical taste. I shared that cold feeling — until a conductor — Kurt Sanderling — who obviously believed in the piece came to my home city as guest and gave a performance of it that convinced me on the spot that the piece had been badly misjudged.

Shostakovich did indeed write a good deal of music that was obviously not intended for the solemn precincts of the concert hall or the Olympian judgments of self-important critics. There are a number of movie scores, some quasi-popular ballets and a good deal of other "occasional" music (including, believe it or not, an orchestration of Vincent Youmans' Tea for Two.) Like Poulenc, among others, he seems at times to have been two composers working in sharply contrasting styles at more or less the same time. .

This may have been a reflection of the double life he was forced to live on the political front, if we can credit the portrait that arises from reading Solomon Volkov's book. Shostakovich's life and his work stand as a kind of enigmatic exhibit in the continuing debate over the influence of politics on the arts. That government interference caused him long-lasting misery is obvious. How deeply this undermined his psychic — and even physical — well-being is not yet absolutely a settled matter. Fortunately, with the drastic changes in political climate of recent years, this is a question that can now at least be researched and debated openly and honestly, without any obscurantism arising from political considerations.

The "Shostakovich question" also has, it seems to me, a still wider resonance. What can this whole complex episode tell us about the influence of political considerations on the public's reception of a composer? When a composer and his music become "news," as Shostakovich did during World War 2, how greatly does this color the way in which concertgoers listen to that music? Would the seventh symphony have become such a cause celebre if it had been written in the safety and obscurity of a peacetime composer's private studio? Would it have been hailed as an instant masterpiece, as it was in the 1940s? Would it then have fallen out of favor and been dismissed as a piece of vulgar musico-political propaganda, as it was in the Cold War years?

These questions are unanswerable, but like many unanswerable questions, they may help us to turn up important truths while we search for "un-answers." Certainly there were other Soviet composers whose music had a certain vogue in the west during the war—Khrennikov, Kallinikov, Khachaturian, Miaskovsky— but they have pretty much faded from view. Of that whole galaxy, only Shostakovich and Prokofieff remain part of the worldwide standard repertory. Political considerations aside, their music obviously had something that the music of the others on that list lacked.

People — even seasoned concertgoers — do not listen to music in a vacuum. They enter the concert hall from the world around it - a world full of political and social tensions with which they live all the time and about which they have decided views. It is unrealistic to expect them to judge music as politically freighted as that of Shostakovitch was without any reference to the circumstances in which it was written. It takes time for these circumstances to recede in relative importance so the music itself can take center stage.

Maybe we have not quite reached that stage yet with respect to this particular composer; but I suspect he is winning the battle, and I think he should.

XXI. BENJAMIN BRITTEN (1913-1976)

In a previous chapter I quoted Arnold Schoenberg's shrewd remark that despite the musical revolution in which he was a chief instigator, "there is still a lot to be said in C major." No composer whose career postdated Schoenberg's has demonstrated the truth of that statement better than Benjamin Britten. He accomplished something that may not appear remarkable or difficult until you think about it a little. He successfully forged a very modern and very personal musical language with roots in the old tonal system rather than in any of the experimental systems devised in the belief that tonality was dead.

This is no small accomplishment. There are fashionable and political pressures and currents in the arts as in all sorts of other fields; it takes a strong personality to resist them and simply to go ones own way, write what one feels one has to write, and let the arbiters of trends be damned. Britten accomplished this and has taken his deserved place as one of the great composers of this century.

It is tempting to compare his career, for example, with that of Gian-Carlo Menotti, who tried to do the same thing but never achieved anything like the degree of respect among critics and fellow musicians that Britten won for himself. This is not to make any judgment on the relative value of the two composers' work, but the comparison is tempting, if only because both men strove, with greatly different results, to make a major impact on the opera stage.

It is true that in a few works Britten did flirt rather gingerly with twelve-tone procedures, but it was never central to his aesthetic. His reputation was made independently of it.

This assessment of Britten's career as a man who simply chose to follow his own inner promptings rather than suit his style to whatever may have been "fashionable" at a given moment places him in distinguished company indeed. It also illuminates one of the salient artistic dilemmas of our time — a dilemma that has been around for a long time surely, but one that has never been so central to our artistic life as it is today.

There have always been composers who simply wrote what they felt in their gut, whether it was fashionable to do so or not. Some of them (Beethoven, Mahler) made it into the accepted pantheon of greats. Others (Schoenberg) are still waiting on the marble steps outside. Still others, of course, have disappeared without a trace.

This pressure to conform to popular fashions is far greater today than it was in any past epoch of musical history. The rise of musical media arbiters and the vast changes in the economic facts of creative life have made this inevitable. It is an especially strong influence on the creator who likes to eat three times a day.

Of course, the courage to write according to your own convictions rather than society's whims is no guarantee of quality. You can still feel that way and be a mediocre composer.

Benjamin Britten was no mediocre composer. He took the gamble and won. As I write, he has been dead for 20 years, but his place in the repertory — both symphonic and operatic, and even in chamber music and vocal music — seems assured. He has been a familiar name on concert and opera bills, and in record shops, for over half a century. With the arguable exception of Ralph Vaughn Williams he is the only English composer mainly identified with the 20th century to have established himself in the repertory so firmly.

There is another potential career pitfall to be considered in Britten's case, too. In some ways it is the exact opposite of the one just discussed.

By rooting his style in the traditional musical speech of an era just past, Britten risked the scorn of critics not for his independence but for his old-fashionedness. It is always easy to dismiss someone as backward looking or unadventurous if his work shows clear connections to the past, and Britten has not escaped that accusation from certain avant-garde quarters. If you are not on the cutting edge of avant-garde experiment, the indictment reads, you're really nobody. It takes a certain amount of courage to resist this sort of pressure from the musical gatekeepers of the day.

Standing right in the middle of all this, of course, is that ultimate arbiter, those who pay at the box-office and go to hear the concerts, who buy the records or who take their music-via-radio seriously enough to listen intelligently. I think it obvious by now that they have ruled decisively (and I think correctly) in Britten's favor. They don't always perform so well, and they too are subject to all sorts of irrelevant but well-nigh-irresistible pressures, but they got this one dead right.

Britten happened along at a fortuitous moment in the history of English musical composition. The Elgar-Delius-Holst generation was gone (all three men died in 1934) and the country was looking for someone to take their place as England's representative on the world musical stage (this is a peculiar trait of the English, it would seem; they always seem to be in search of someone they can point to as their "great composer" before the world. Britten certainly filled the bill admirably, but others have not been so lucky: the young Arthur Sullivan was overborne by the idea and went on, almost against his will, to make himself immortal in the field of operetta; other quite respectable talents like Sterndale Bennett, Parry and Stanford, simply could not measure up to the overpraise of their countrymen. At the moment the reputation of Sir Michael Tippett hangs in the international balance).

Britten has become known perhaps most widely as a composer for the voice, and there is no doubt that he has left a large and treasurable legacy of vocal music, not only in opera but also in the song-cycle, the cantata and various other forms. One of his strong claims to front-rank status is simply that he has done so well in such a wide variety of media — in opera, in choral music, purely orchestral works, chamber music, solo-instrument-with-orchestra pieces, music for children and for films, and in one or two genres that he more or less invented himself, like his series of "parables for church performance," the best known of which is the superb Curlew River.

This is not necessarily the infallible sign of a great composer — one could easily adduce lots of contrary examples — but it is the sign of a thorough professional, of a man who knew his craft and plied it with practiced mastery. Verdi, Wagner and Puccini were not necessarily lesser composers just because they devoted their energies almost exclusively to opera, nor was Chopin somehow a lesser figure because he wrote almost exclusively for the piano; but the achievements of a Britten, a Richard Strauss, or a Mozart in so many different media mark them as a special type, the fully rounded master composer.

Britten first came to true international celebrity at the end of World War 2, with the premiere of his great opera Peter Grimes, hailed from the night of its premiere in 1945 as a masterpiece and still a common item on the world's stages. It set the stylistic terms for much of what was to follow in Britten's output with the decorative yet wonderfully expressive quality of its vocal writing, in the boldness and pictorial vividness of its orchestration, in the composer's sensitivity to both the meaning and sound of words and in the opera's sheer dramatic effectiveness. Grimes himself, the lonely, somewhat surly and misunderstood fisherman, was an unlikely sort of operatic hero — a man almost inarticulate except when dreaming to himself, as in his weirdly beautiful entrance aria in the pub scene ("Now the Great Bear and Pleiades...")

The love interest between Grimes and Ellen Orford is never really developed in the opera. It remains a somewhat pale side issue. Britten thus deliberately deprived himself of one of the most common and dependable of operatic audience-involvement devices. Here again he chose to go a different and much more difficult way — to involve the audience in the drama not through the love of a man for a woman, but through the more abstract idea of the conflict of a man with society. Grimes was but the first of a whole series of heroes in Britten's operas to whom this idea might be applied. "The Borough" (the name taken over from the title of the narrative poem by George Crabbe on which the opera is based) is collectively a character in the opera, its collective persona broken up by Britten and his librettist into a memorable series of minor-character vignettes —

ranting religious fanatic, oily attorney, pompous mayor, old maid drug addict, etc. — by contrast with whom Grimes achieves heroic stature in spite of his obviously unheroic character. Britten went on after that early triumph to produce a wide variety of strikingly original operas: chamber works for smaller forces (Albert Herring, The Turn of the Screw, The Rape of Lucretia,) a celebratory work for a royal coronation (Gloriana), an opera conceived for television (Owen Wingrave) works on daringly unconventional themes (Death in Venice, Billy Budd), operas for children (Noye's Fludde, The Little Sweep), and his striking Shakespeare opera A Midsummer Night's Dream. With perhaps the exception of Gloriana they are all still around - performed with fair frequency on the world's opera stages and readily available on records. (And let me confess a personal quirk of taste: I find Britten's operatic version of Turn of the Screw infinitely more arresting than its source, the famous novella by Henry James.)

There is also the powerful and unconventional War Requiem, a large-scale oratorio that combines the Latin text of the Catholic mass with the antiwar poetry of Wilfred Owen. This strikingly original piece marks an intersection of Britten's professional and personal lives, for it gives expression to the pacifist convictions that the composer held all his life.

Among his other non-operatic vocal music, one may single out the exquisite Serenade for tenor, solo horn and strings, a truly lovely setting of six first-rate poems on the common theme of death. I have remarked earlier that much of the world's great vocal music was composed to less than the greatest texts. No one would contend that all the poetry so beautifully set to music by Schubert came from the top drawer of our poetic treasure-chest, for example. The Britten Serenade, however, is an example of beautiful music wedded to absolutely first-rate poetry by major poets (and I make no apology for the fact that Tennyson is one of them). A number of Britten's other song cycles are well worth knowing, especially the early but truly beautiful Les Illuminations.

Among Britten's nonvocal instrumental music (the list is not particularly large) one may single out the early but ingenious Variations on the Theme of Frank Bridge, the curious Sinfonia da Requiem and the well-known Young Person's Guide to the Orchestra as especially attractive pieces. The adjective "curious" as applied to the Sinfonia da Requiem refers to the work's unusual history — commissioned by the Japanese government to celebrate the 2,600th anniversary of the founding of the Mikado's dynasty, the piece was summarily rejected by the Japanese because of its use of titles drawn from Christian religious ritual, which the non-Christian sponsors found inappropriate. Britten was taken aback but let the work stand in his catalogue anyway, and it has had a good number of performances and recordings over the years.

Britten has produced a fair amount of expertly crafted chamber music over the years, but it is (unfairly) neglected by our performance industry these days. The Phantasy Quartet for oboe and strings is a good example.

One word that applies pretty well to Britten's output in general is that loaded term "accessible." This simply means music that is likely to make an appeal right away to the serious listener, even though he may not have any great background in what we call so glibly "modern music." It may sound new and "different," but because it has hearable roots in the musical past the listener is able to make a connection, to get Britten's message and to enjoy what he hears.

In some quarters to call a piece "accessible" is a term of covert condemnation, a coded judgment that the composer has somehow written down to the audience and is not to be taken really seriously. I once appeared on a public panel discussion with, among other people, a well-known avant-garde composer. Someone in the audience made the mistake of asking a question that included the term "music of the masses," and the composer quickly fired back a verbal guided missile: "I'm not concerned with 'music of the masses.' The masses have their music — their Beatles, their My Fair Lady and their Benjamin Britten." That stopped the questioner dead in his tracks, but it left me thinking long and hard about the mind-set that it represented. Contemplate for a moment the plight of the poor music critic (my own lot for 28 years) who must deal with such ideas and controversies in as fair-minded a way as he can manage.

Benjamin Britten succeeded far better than most in establishing himself successfully in the no-man's land between public acceptance and avant-garde experimentation. His music speaks with a voice that is at once individual, challenging and beautiful. It is no sin to speak a musical language that people can understand without the need to consult a guidebook full of technical jargon.

In this respect you could draw an interesting parallel between Britten's career and that of his exact contemporary, the American composer Samuel Barber. Both men suffered in some quarters for their popularity with a fairly wide swath of the musical public; yet neither man has established himself firmly at the center of the popular standard repertory (though Britten is coming steadily closer as time goes on.)

Both men were basically conservatives in a musical age that looked suspiciously at people who wore that label. It is a little ironic that since their deaths (Britten in 1976, Barber in 1981), the so-called "romantic revival" has set in; composers and public are returning to a more tonally oriented, expressive and openly communicative musical style. There is an old saw among the nonmusical that says immortality is only conferred upon long-dead composers, and sometimes one is ruefully compelled to think that maybe there is a grain of truth in the idea.

The jury is still out on Samuel Barber, but I feel safe in predicting that Britten has won his case and that his music will be around for us to enjoy for the foreseeable future. He speaks the language of emotion and communication with a distinctive accent, but his speech is understood — and, more important, he has a lot to say to us.